COPING WITH
CHILDREN'S MISBEHAVIOR

COPING WITH CHILDREN'S MISBEHAVIOR

A Parent's Guide

by Rudolf Dreikurs, M.D.

HAWTHORN BOOKS, INC.

PUBLISHERS / *New York*

COPING WITH CHILDREN'S MISBEHAVIOR

Library of Congress Catalog Card Number: 72-1398

ISBN: 0-8015-1764-8

7 8 9 10

Coping with Children's Misbehavior: A Parent's Guide and *The Challenge of Child Training: A Parent's Guide*, also by Rudolf Dreikurs, previously appeared together as *The Challenge of Parenthood*.

Contents

PART I
UNDERSTANDING THE CHILD

Introduction

If it were possible to rear children properly from birth on, if parents were faultless and the atmosphere in which children grew up were completely harmonious, then extreme misbehavior, violation of order, and maladjustment would probably not occur. But since these favorable conditions rarely exist, children cause an infinite variety of difficulties. It helps little to talk of what should have been done from the beginning to avoid the predicament; it is necessary to guide parents and children to a solution of their *existing* problems.

You cannot help your child unless you understand him. This complete lack of understanding is one of the tragedies of contemporary parent-child relationships. Most parents have not the slightest idea of why the child misbehaves; they are completely ignorant of the causes and purposes of his actions. In the following cases we will try to demonstrate why and to what end a child behaves as he does. You will perceive the concept on which he has built his existence. This may help you to recognize the life plan that guides his actions. Then you may realize the difficulties that confront *him*. So far you have probably been impressed only with the difficulties that *you* have had with him. It is only when you have an appreciation of his conflicts that you can really help him to resolve them.

In order to be able to exert a constructive influence on your child you must learn to observe him objectively. This you can do only if you take his misbehavior less seriously. You must stop regarding his faults as a moral issue. The child who misbehaves is not a "bad" child. He is only unhappy, misguided, and discouraged, and has not found the right answer to the social problems which confront him. Every misbehavior indicates an error of judgment in his efforts to find his place within the family and to meet the demands and pressures to which he is subjected.

As parents rarely understand his concept and judgment, they are puzzled by the way in which he tries to solve his problems. Often a mother recites with complete bewilderment and moral indignation the various misdeeds, deficiencies, and transgressions of her child. "How can he do that? Look what he did again!" Her account cannot be interpreted intelligently at its face value; the child's behavior makes sense only when one knows the counterpart played by parents or other leading figures in his environment. Action and reaction are completely logical on both sides and equally faulty in a psychological sense. The real issue is not a moral one but a question of personal interrelationships. The moral note is raised by the parents merely as a tool to defend their defeated authority (a misinterpretation which society as a whole is prone to make). Thus the intrinsic, disturbed relationship is veiled and the problem is diverted to one of judgment, which is supposed to be objective. Such an attitude makes the educational problem static and unsolvable.

Every action of a child has a purpose which is in line with his effort toward social integration. A well-behaved and well-adjusted child has found his way toward social acceptance by conforming with the rules governing the social group in which he lives. He senses the requirements of the group and acts accordingly. He is active when the situation warrants it and passive when need be; he talks at the proper time and knows when to be quiet. He can be a leader or a follower. A perfectly adjusted child—if there ever was one!—would reveal little individuality; he would merely reflect the social needs of his environment. Only in the slight deviation from perfect adjustment, through the characteristic approaches which he has found and developed for himself, does a child manifest his individual personality.

In this sense, all individual activity implies a slight deviation from absolute conformity. We cannot consider this deviation as maladjustment because the needs of any social group are not static. The social group itself requires improvement, growth, and evolution. The individual who imposes his ideas on the group is the impetus for its development. If his ideas are beneficial for the group and his method constructive, he is still—and only then—well adjusted, although not completely conforming. Thus, mere conformity can be an obstacle to social development and thereby can become an expression of social maladjustment.

Maladjustment can be defined as behavior which disturbs the functioning of the group and its evolution. The psychological dynamics underlying maladjustment in adults are very complex. It takes time and great effort to unveil the variety of factors at work beyond consciousness, and the mask of adulthood. Adults have the same fundamental attitudes which they had as children; but in the process of adolescence they learn for appearance's sake to cover up and to accept the pattern set by society. The successful masking of one's intentions and motivations is then called maturity. The child has not yet reached this stage of development; although he, too, is not aware of his goals and intentions, he demonstrates his attitudes openly. It is possible, therefore, to recognize the goals of a child's behavior merely by observation.

All disturbing behavior of the child is directed toward one of four possible goals. They represent his ideas about his relationship to others in the group. He tries to: (1) gain attention; (2) demonstrate his power; (3) punish or get even; (4) demonstrate his inadequacy.

A child's goal may occasionally vary with circumstance; he may act to attract attention at one moment, and assert his power or seek revenge at another. It is usually possible to tell by the child's behavior whether his predominant goal is attention, power, or revenge, or whether he is trying to evade any action and responsibility by demonstrating to the outside world, and proving to himself, his inadequacy. He may resort to different techniques to obtain his ends, and the same behavior pattern can be used for different purposes.

The attention-getting mechanism (A.G.M.) is operative in most young children. It is the result of the method in which children are brought up in our culture. Young children have very few opportunities to establish their social position through useful contribution. There is so little that they are permitted to contribute to the welfare and the needs of the family. Older siblings and adults do everything that has to be done. The only way a young child can feel accepted and a part of his family group is through the older members of the family. *Their* contributions give *him* value and social status. As a result, the child seeks constant proof of his acceptance through gifts, demonstrations of affection, or at least through attention. As none of these increases his own feeling of strength, self-reliance, and self-confidence, the child requires constant new proof lest he feel lost and rejected. He will try to get what he wants in socially acceptable ways as long as possible. However, when he loses confidence in his ability to use socially constructive means effectively, he will try any conceivable method of putting others into his service or of getting attention. Unpleasant effects like humiliation, punishment, or even physical pain do not matter so long as the main purpose is achieved. Children prefer being beaten to being ignored. If a child is ignored and treated with indifference he feels definitely excluded, rejected, and without any place with the group.

The desire for attention can be satisfied through constructive methods. The child is naturally inclined to be constructive as long as he feels able to succeed. However, if his requests become excessive or if the environment refuses to meet his demands, the child may discover that he gets more attention by disturbing. Then the struggle starts. For a while the parents may succumb to the provocation without getting too angry and annoyed. Pleasant and unpleasant episodes are held in balance: the child's desire to occupy his parents with himself is met and a workable equilibrium is maintained. However, there may come a time when the parents decide to subdue the child, to stop him from being annoying and disturbing. Then the child changes his goal and he and the parents become deadlocked in a struggle for power and superiority. The child tries to impress upon the parents that he can do what he wants and that they are powerless to stop him. Or he may demonstrate to them in a passive way that they cannot force him to do what they want. If he gets away with it, he has won a victory; if the parents enforce their will, he has lost; but he will come back the next time with stronger methods. This struggle is more fierce than his fight for attention. The child's maladjustment is more obvious, his actions are more hostile and the emotions involved more violent.

This battle between parents and child for power and dominance may reach a point where the parents resort to every conceivable means to subjugate the culprit. The mutual antagonism and hatred may become so strong that no pleasant experience remains to sustain a feeling of belonging, of friendliness or cooperation. The child moves then to the third goal: he no longer hopes for attention, his effort to gain power seems hopeless, he feels completely ostracized and disliked, and finds his only gratification in hurting others and avenging his own hurt. That seems to him the only alternative. "At least, I can make them hate me," is his despairing motto. In groups where he can still gain personal superiority and power he may act less violent and cruel than in those where he has lost every status. Children of this type are the most violent and vicious; they know where it hurts most and take advantage of the vulnerability of their opponents. No display of power and force impresses them any longer. They are defiant and destructive. As they are convinced from the beginning that nobody likes them, they provoke anyone with whom they come in contact to reject them. They regard it as a triumph when they are considered horrible; that is the only triumph they can obtain, the only one they seek.

A passive child will not move in the direction of open warfare. If his antagonism is successfully beaten down, he may be discouraged to such an extent that he cannot hope for any significance whatsoever. Similar conclusions may be reached by a child who considers attention-getting or power as essential, and finds himself unable to obtain it. Then he gives up in discouragement and refuses participation and functioning. There seems to be no sense in doing anything if it will bring only defeat and failure. This defeat, then, looms as the greatest danger, and the child tries his best to avoid it, by proving his inadequacy to himself and others. He uses his inability as a protection so that nothing should be required or expected of him. In this way he tries to avoid more humiliating and embarrassing experiences.

Maladjusted children may be either active or passive and in either case they may use constructive or destructive methods. The choice of method depends on the child's feeling of being accepted or rejected by groups of people: his antagonism is always expressed in destructive acts. This feeling of belonging or the lack of it is a decisive factor for the switch from constructive to destructive methods. Active or passive behavior indicates the amount of courage the child possesses. Passivity is always based on personal discouragement. The combination of the two pairs of factors leads to four types of behavior patterns:

1. Active-constructive

2. Active-destructive
3. Passive-constructive
4. Passive-destructive.

The sequence as presented is based on the actual progression of maladjustment. Many parents and educators are inclined to regard an active-destructive child as much worse than a passive-constructive one. However, this is not necessarily true. If the child's antisocial attitude has not developed too far, as in cases of attention-getting, he can be induced with relative ease to change his destructive methods into constructive ones; but it is extremely difficult to change a passive child into an active one. The passive-constructive child is less unpleasant, but needs more assistance for the development of self-confidence and courage.

Attention-getting (goal 1) is the only goal that can be achieved by all four behavior patterns. (For this reason, the various behavior patterns which serve for attention-getting will be divided accordingly, while the other behavior patterns will appear only under the heading of goals 2, 3, and 4, without division into active and passive methods.) Active- and passive-destructive methods can be used for seeking superiority (goal 2) or revenge (goal 3), while the display of inadequacy (goal 4) can naturally use only passive-destructive methods.

A short discussion of the four types of attention-getting mechanisms may help to clarify the point. The *active-constructive* A.G.M. resembles a very cooperative and conforming behavior. The difference is that in this case the good behavior of a child exists only for the purpose of getting attention and recognition: it will turn into misbehavior if the child does not receive the desired attention. Then he may try *active-destructive* methods. This type of behavior may resemble that used to achieve the second or third goal, and distinguishes itself from it only by the lack of violence and antagonism. The child still seeks only attention and the fight stops when this goal is achieved. The child who wants to demonstrate his power is not satisfied with mere attention; he wants his way.

A very interesting group is that which uses *passive-constructive* methods for attention-getting. Many parents and teachers do not recognize the actions of children in this group as misbehavior. Their pleasantness, charm, and submission cause the observer to overlook the discouragement behind their passivity and dependence on others. In the masculine culture, passive-constructive behavior patterns are almost demanded from women. For this reason, the passive-constructive A.G.M. is found more frequently in girls than in boys. We have already pointed out the mistaken tendency to overlook the greater discouragement of *passive-constructive* children as compared with the *active-destructive*. The passive-constructive child is less unpleasant, but needs more assistance for the development of self-confidence and courage. A child who seeks attention with passive-destructive methods may very well end up in the fourth group of completely discouraged children.

Part I will be devoted to an *understanding* of the child's problems, but a few general principles for treatment of the various groups and types can be formulated. Children who drive for attention must learn to become independent by recognizing that *contributing* and not *receiving* is the effective instrument for obtaining social status. Within the four groups of A.G.M., the attempt should be made to help all children to become active and to change destructive methods into constructive ones, until the child is able to overcome the need for any special attention. Children who drive for power and superiority should not be exposed to power and to pressure against which they have successfully rebelled and still rebel. Acknowledging their value and even their power is essential for making them self-confident so that they may no longer need their power drive. They must learn that power is less important than being useful. Children who want to punish and to get even are usually those who are convinced that nobody likes them or ever will like them. Helping them involves a long process of demonstrating that they are or can be liked. Children who give up in discouragement have to be brought back slowly to the realization of their abilities and potentialities.

The various behavior difficulties which children present do not necessarily indicate the pursuit of one and the same goal. Laziness, for instance, can well be employed for all four. It can serve either to get attention and assistance, or to establish superiority by refusing what has to be done, or as revenge against an overambitious parent who thereby becomes personally hurt. Or it can be used as an excuse when it seems hopeless to gain anything by trying.

In the following discussions the various behavior problems will be arranged as accurately as possible according to the one goal for which they are most frequently used. But the fact that a given problem appears under one heading need not mean that it could not show itself in other circumstances or for other purposes as well.

The main emphasis will be placed on the clarification of the relationships between the child and his parents and siblings as the basis for the understanding of his behavior. For the purpose of convenient reference, some of the material will be repetitious, especially in regard to possible techniques in dealing with each problem, which will be indicated only briefly; these short suggestions will necessarily be similar for those problems with similar psychological mechanisms.

CHAPTER 1

Attention-Getting Mechanism

ACTIVE-CONSTRUCTIVE METHODS

The "Model" Child

Many children who are the sheer delight of their parents and teachers are actually not so perfect as they seem to be. They merely try very hard to display their "goodness" to gain praise and recognition. Their lack of genuine goodness becomes apparent under certain circumstances. They often have a poor social relationship to their own age group; if they cannot shine, they feel lost. Their desire to be perfect, to be correct, to be superior is often stimulated by overambitious and perfectionistic parents who encourage such traits, sometimes in playing this particular child against other siblings. Competition with a sibling often leads to the development of this striving for applause. In order to maintain his superiority over a younger brother or sister, or to match and possibly exceed an older sibling, the child tries to become good, reliable, considerate, cooperative, and industrious, seeking and accepting any possible responsibility. Little do he and his parents realize how his excellence affects the other sibling, driving the latter into discouragement and maladjustment. The virtue of the model child is only too frequently achieved at the expense of the problem child.

Nine-year-old Billy was a wonderful little boy. He had lost his father four years ago, and he managed to be a great solace and help to his mother. Very early he assisted her not only in housework, but also in taking care of six-year-old Marilyn. Even at his tender age, mother could discuss any problem with him, and he actually assumed the function of the "man of the family." The only area in which Billy did not do so well was at school. He had few friends and was not particularly interested in schoolwork. That is not surprising when we consider that in school Billy could not attain the extraordinary position which he enjoyed at home.

One can easily imagine what type of child Marilyn was. She was so unruly that mother no longer knew how to manage her and asked for help. She was untidy, unreliable, noisy, disturbing, and annoying, a real "brat." Mother could not understand how the two children could be so different! It was hard for her to realize the connection between Billy's goodness and Marilyn's deficiencies.

We had the following discussion with both children together: First, we asked Marilyn whether she thought mother liked her. As could be expected, her answer was a shaking of the head. Then we explained to her that mother loved her very much. But because she, Marilyn, did not believe it, she acted in such a way as to make mother constantly angry with her. Perhaps she thought mother would pay attention to her only when she misbehaved. If she would try to behave differently, she would learn that mother loved her, too.

We then asked Billy whether he wanted Marilyn to be a good and nice girl. He immediately shouted, "No!" We asked him why and he became embarrassed, groped for an answer, and finally said, "She won't be good, anyhow." Then we explained to him that perhaps we could help her; and he could help her, too. Together we might succeed in making her a good girl. Would he like that? Somewhat uncertainly he said, yes, he would like it. I told him frankly I did not believe he meant it seriously; I was sure that his first "no" was more sincere and accurate. But why didn't he want her to be good? Perhaps he could tell me. He was thoughtful for a while. And then it came out—"Because I want to be better."

Such children do not enjoy being good if they are not recognized as being better than others. And they actually stop being good if they cannot be better, as happened to Billy at school. If we succeed in helping the difficult child, the so-called good one generally becomes troublesome, sometimes for the first time in his life. For this reason it is not sufficient to adjust the problem child. The whole relationship must be improved. Billy needs as much encouragement as does Marilyn. He, too, is not sure of his position and is afraid of losing it. His desire to be so good is simply a compensation for the fundamental doubt in himself.

Frequently a younger child makes up for his deficiency in age and strength by using his goodness as a tool for superiority to gain the interest and favor of his parents. Sometimes girls compensate for the privileges and prerogatives of their brothers by becoming extremely considerate and responsible, to the detriment of their male competitors, who become more unreliable and selfish as they cannot keep up with the goodness of their sister. Such "goodness" of a girl may endanger her own happiness and ability to get along with others, because—without being aware of it—she makes others feel like a heel; she may make herself a door-mat for everybody willing to step on her. That gives her a peculiar glory of moral superiority. In this way she may become a martyr, always blaming her own misery on the deficiencies of others. Because her maladjustment is seldom recognized in time, no efforts are made to help such a "good" girl.

Exaggerated Conscientiousness

Overconscientiousness is often employed as a technique to gain approval and to demonstrate one's moral superiority over other children. Behind exaggerated conscience lies the strife for special attention—generally hidden from everyone, and not realized even by the child himself. As long as attention and recognition are obtained, as long as parents submit to the child's demand for constant approval and reassurance, conformity is maintained. But sooner or later the child's method will be challenged, either when the parents refuse to submit any longer to his exaggerated demands, or when siblings or playmates revolt against the special consideration which he gets.

This extreme conscience may then be used in an active-destructive way, and is then used for the purpose of getting more power and superiority, even over the parents. Unusual ambition and a great ability to rationalize can move a child to cloak his striving for superiority and power as overconscientiousness. He does everything asked of him, but in such a way that the opposite is accomplished, with the result that the parent, against whom the conflict may be directed, flies into a helpless rage. Yet everything is glossed over with affection and good will. He drives his parents to distraction with his immoderate and compulsive efforts to do everything outstandingly well. He is not unclean—far from it! He washes his hands thirty times a day, and thus dawdles away his time. He is late to meals for the same reason, has to interrupt his studies, and is tardy at school. The excessive love of order conceals a struggle *against* order. He is not lazy—on the contrary, he works the whole day long, so that he has to be stopped or sent to bed. And if you take him from his studies and put him to bed, he is naturally unprepared the next day and fails in the test. Like any form of hidden antagonism, this attitude favors the growth of a neurosis.

You should not be deceived about the hostile nature of the child's behavior or let yourself be drawn into conflict with him by attempting to intervene forcibly in his affairs. Urging and admonishing, not to speak of threats, are either without effect or only intensify the struggle for power. It is necessary to recognize the causes of the hostile attitude and of the child's rebellion. For the most part, they have their origin in extravagant pampering and/or high pressure on the parents' part. The child has no faith in himself, nor in the people around him. Thus he stresses his good intentions and excuses his defects.

Eleven-year-old Mary is an overconscientious child. Her parents, extremely loving and anxious, were always fretting over their only child. They studied her moods, anticipated her every desire, dogged her footsteps, and took elaborate care that she should not overtax herself. It was only natural that she, from a healthy instinct, should rise up against this extreme solicitude. Idolizing her parents as she did, she could not give open expression to her revolt. But she caused them a great deal of unhappiness by taking everything in deadly earnest and regretting deeply each of her own slips and errors. And as a consequence, she made far more mistakes than could be explained by mere ineptitude. Whatever she was asked to do became a problem; and soon her parents were wary of asking anything of her.

Parents may become irritable and perhaps even harsh if they rebel against the exaggerated moral values of the child. In this event, the child will not yield to pressure nor give up his moral convictions and good will, but will increase his inner defiance to a point of complete inner isolation. In his behavior he may then resemble a highly stubborn and defiant child, distinguishing himself from an openly rebellious child only by the maintenance of his "good intentions."

Bright Sayings

A good many children are conspicuous because of their ability to express themselves in a striking and amusing way. Whatever they have to say is charming. The parents tend to brag about their offspring's "bright" and "cute" remarks to their acquaintances, usually without considering whether or not the child is present when they boast about him. He, naturally enough, rejoices in his prowess and starts to turn out bright remarks on a big scale. While the child is small, his utterances may have a certain charm, if only through the quaintness of his speech and the unspoiled power of observation that children evince. But gradually pertness may become a plague, and amusement yield to dismay. Now, instead of helping the child out of the difficult situation in which their own awkwardness has involved him, instead of bringing him around in a friendly fashion and diverting his desire for recognition into other more acceptable channels, the parents begin to chide and scold. It is most disastrous to label him as a "jabber-jabber," a "chatterbox," for his development will become definitely fixed in this direction.

The urge to talk arises from a striving for recognition. It reveals anxiety. Naturally the tendency is most pronounced in those who find it hard to assert themselves more constructively. The greater volubility of women is probably owing to this cause. Tattling, a specialized form of the same fault, likewise serves to raise a feeling of personal prestige. It is very difficult to keep small children from blurting out confidences, for they know all too well that they can be sensational by saying precisely that which should be left unsaid. You must understand this temptation and not blame the child too severely for his transgressions. But you may easily train him to discretion by presenting it as a high attainment, a proof that he is already grown up. By this means the child may discover silence as more desirable than talking. Mere exhortations, however, and especially reproofs, will never touch the fundamental reasons for talkativeness.

ACTIVE-DESTRUCTIVE METHODS
Showing Off

Ambitious children who are discouraged in the field of tangible, useful achievement, may use the most bizarre means to put themselves in the foreground and attract attention.

Eight-year-old Irving had a sister three years older than he. She was energetic and capable, learned easily, and at eleven already looked quite grown up. The boy was delicate and small, but very aggressive. He always had the last word and was constantly showing off. At school he was extremely restless and inattentive, and disturbed the class with his antics and gesticulations.

How did the parents react to this tendency to attract attention? They regarded him as vain and difficult to please, and usually attempted to suppress his obvious striving for recognition. Such efforts, naturally enough, were in vain, for the child was really discouraged, and disparagement only strengthened his poor opinion of himself. He gave the appearance of being unambitious, since he made little effort to learn, and accepted punishments or censure at school with apparent indifference. In reality he was highly ambitious; but his ambition was not directed toward useful attainments. This approach was blocked for him by his sister. She had crowded Irving into the background.

Irving must realize that he does not always have to be the center of attention to compensate for his sister's superiority. His exaggerated opinion of her importance and doubts about his own position are further confirmed by the dissatisfaction that he arouses through his misguided attempts to assert himself. He must, therefore, be shown that he is not only esteemed for what he can do, but also that he is loved. Hitherto he has experienced his importance only when he succeeded in shocking people. This practice can be stopped. Occasional experiences of an inexorable order are as necessary when he misbehaves as attention and interest when he behaves well.

Obtrusiveness

Innumerable are the tricks by which children try to impress others. The weird ideas that occur to them are often astounding and amusing. Innocent parents who have no conception of the reasons behind such conduct are often completely bewildered—when, for instance, their four-year-old boy (the youngest of the family) takes a notion to cut his soup with his knife! The child's tendency to attract attention frequently takes the form of "bedeviling" the grown-ups. In this way he makes his presence felt and keeps his family on edge. He interrupts his parents' conversations; he refuses to let his mother talk with acquaintances.

Eight-year-old Gertrude—a second-born, spoiled child—would not allow her mother to pay attention to anyone else when she was around. If the mother wanted to talk with someone else, Gertrude put her hand over her mother's mouth or yelled so loudly that conversation was impossible. Between screams and protests she clung to her mother's neck and kissed her profusely. Her wildness and turbulence made her the terror of nursemaids. At school, however, she worked so hard that her diligence seemed to justify overlooking her less estimable traits. She was the "teacher's pet" and the best student in the class. She knew that at school she would not succeed with her tricks.

The "Walking Question Mark"

A child may annoy not only with persistent and unwarranted displays of affection; he may also make himself conspicuous through questioning. You can easily determine whether he asks for information or only in order to call attention to himself. You should not refuse to answer truthfully an honest query; but it is entirely out of place to discuss sham questions. The latter are clearly characterized by the way in which the child puts his questions. He pays no attention, and sometimes does not even wait for a response before asking a new question. Parents often fail to notice this game. They do not even catch on when the same questions are frequently repeated. When their patience is exhausted they brusquely scold the child, who is amazed at this sudden turn in the conversation and really hurt.

Once at the home of a friend I watched the following scene. The mother took her little three-year-old daughter on her lap and read to her from a picture book. On each page the girl stopped the mother and asked "What are these people doing?" and "Why is this dog here?" And each time the mother answered patiently. After a few pages I broke in and asked "What are these people doing?" and the little girl answered correctly! I kept quiet while the next page was being read and the child asked one or two questions, which the mother again answered patiently. This was the sequence: during the reading of one page I asked the questions and the child answered; during the reading of the next page the child asked and the mother answered, and so on. After the mother finished the book, I remarked that I had enjoyed the game. The mother asked in astonishment, "What game?" She had noticed nothing at all of what was going on.

This episode is less humorous than deplorable. It shows how little parents are aware of the tricks of their children and thereby encourage false attention-getting mechanisms. This little girl called three or four times after she was put to bed; for water, toilet, a running nose, and a forgotten item—and the parents complied until they became irritated. This is the usual sad end of such a game.

You should not let a child get away with *thoughtless* questions. By listening carefully it will not be hard to distinguish these from serious inquiries. But you must realize that children sometimes enlarge their mental horizons with startling abruptness, and then they actually have a great store of sincere questions. However, it is still possible to differentiate between a thoughtful and a purely mechanical spinning out of questions: the latter is often marked by the stereotyped form or the general senselessness of the queries. The eternal "Why?" of children may spring from a real thirst for knowledge; but more often it shows only the desire to attract attention. Even when you have determined that the latter is the case, you should not react with reprimands. You can remind the child that he cannot possibly be in earnest with his queries.

This can be done in all friendliness. He will soon stop his tedious questioning when it fails to bring the desired result. If you answer such questions at all, your reply should not be logical—as the child already knows the answer. You may play a little game with him. It often works when you agree to ask questions alternately, first the child, then you; or, you can shoot questions at him in the same way he does; or you may make up a fantastic story to answer a simple question. But all such games should be introduced properly, explaining to the child why he asks the questions, and expressing your willingness to give him your attention if he wants it. If you have no time at the moment, you can say that you will give him your answer later. You do not save time if you answer logically to keep him quiet, or say "I don't know"—which is not true; or if you shout at him and try to stop him. All such responses will only stimulate him to bother you further with his questions.

Once more we must emphasize that questions arising from the child's need to expand his knowledge should never be ignored or ridiculed. Disparagement leads to forfeiting the child's confidence and drives him to other sources of information. Or it may hamper his intellectual development. A child who asks a question objectively and seriously is generally capable of grasping a simple reply. You should never tell him that he is too young to understand. You must take the trouble to discover the real gist of the question; and if the answer is limited strictly to the question, it will not exceed the bounds of the child's understanding. An adult may perhaps regard a child's question as unanswerable, and believe that it passes the child's power of comprehension merely because he, the grown-up, thinks at once of the additional questions that would arise from an exact reply. The child, however, queries no deeper than he can think. (This, of course, applies only to serious questions.)

In addition to objective and obtrusive questions are the so-called rhetorical questions: "Is that right?" "Is that what you really believe?" "Do you mean it?" "Do you think so?" Any reply to such queries is, at best, inept, and in any case unwarranted. But, nevertheless, critical, scolding parents often use such questions as an occasion for harsh or at least unfriendly comments.

"Enfant Terrible"

The ability to say or do something at exactly the wrong time characterizes the "enfant terrible." His purpose is to draw attention to himself under every circumstance, and he succeeds in the simplest way: by breaking the unwritten laws of tact and convention whenever he can. Often these children are especially attractive because of their intelligence and wit, and the charm with which they dramatize themselves. Their strategy is to do nothing that is expressly forbidden but to carry the permissible to extremes.

Eight-year-old Francis was an "enfant terrible." He had lost his parents and was being reared, with more determination than good sense, by two older brothers and an older sister. He was pulled back and forth between their sympathetic indulgence and their helpless severity. But he knew how to attract everyone's attention. Once his brother scolded him severely for telling a lie and delivered an extemporaneous sermon on the necessity of truthfulness, with astounding results. The following day a distant relative paid a call; Francis informed him at once that the family spoke of him in no complimentary terms. He answered the subsequent reproaches of sister and brothers with the ingenuous comment that after all one must always tell the truth. And henceforth no one could rid him of this hyper-veracity. His family trembled whenever a guest arrived; they knew that Francis, with uncanny skill, would dig up something embarrassing but true to tell.

Naturally, an "enfant terrible" who is worthy of the name does not limit himself to embarrassing remarks. He plays his tricks in infinite variety and with remarkable inventive faculty.

Once in our Child Guidance Center, I became the victim of my own gullibility. A little girl, about five, appeared for the first time during our consultation hour. The mother told of the child's pranks and of her own efforts to influence her through pleading, which of course remained fruitless. Meanwhile the girl sat on a bench and played perilously with the inkwell. Her mother warned her and pulled her hand away, but it did no good. Now I was eager to show how it should be done; so I said, "Go ahead and put your hand in the ink. You'll just get your fingers dirty, and it won't look very nice. But go ahead and try it if you want to." As I had expected, the child was taken aback by my words and stopped playing with the inkstand. But suddenly, after some ten minutes, I heard a sharp cry from the mother. The girl had thrust both her hands into the inkwell and proudly and exultantly held up her little fists dripping with ink.

It is plain to see that the "enfant terrible" is not easy to reform, for the simple reason that he is sly and clever. Yet the consequences of his conduct in later life are rarely as bad as distracted parents are led to fear, for these children are shrewd enough to calculate when and to what length they can venture a prank. Nevertheless, one should try to deal with them. Naturally, this cannot be done unless parents call off the conflict with them and win their understanding and sympathy, for these children are intelligent enough to recognize the purpose of their behavior. It is not so simple to let them experience the natural consequences, since they themselves—as we have just seen in the case of Francis—are sufficiently adroit to use the unpleasant consequences of their acts to their own ends. Yet suitable opportunities for logical consequences can be found.

In the first place, the child is too often permitted to succeed in his maneuvers. Parents scold him, but they laugh at his tricks; and this, of course, spurs him on to bigger and better achievements of the same sort. Visitors or other outsiders who are only occasional, amused witnesses of such scenes exercise a particularly harmful influence. Hence it is a good idea to deprive the child of the opportunity to show off before guests. You need only say to the child: "Do you think you can behave today when Aunt X comes? Shall we give it a try?" And if he does not act properly, you can keep him out of sight the next two or three times when you have guests. Later you can give him another chance. But in the meantime efforts must be made to win the child over. Above all, you must understand the entire situation, which perhaps involves rivalry with an older brother or sister. You must also avoid paying undue attention to the child or stimulating his ambition to satisfy your own vanity.

Instability

This trait, too, has a definite purpose.

Fourteen-year-old Lil is in constant agitation. She is perpetually changing her clothes, her friends, her activities, her interests;

and she is soon satiated with everything. For a short while she excelled in mathematics; then she turned to history, devoured one fat volume after another, and tossed them aside. She is continually showing how gifted she is—what she *could* do, *if*—if she could only stick to one thing for any length of time. And this is the principle by which she acts.

Lil stands in the shadow of a very capable and conscientious elder brother. Ostensibly she is the more talented of the two. But he accomplishes more and is dependable. So Lil *tries to suggest what she potentially could do.* She has no faith in her ability to fulfill her promises. Not only does she fear disappointments, she actually provokes them. She arranges them everywhere—in her personal relationships, as well as in books and interests. She does not realize that the disillusionments do not come from outside, but grow within herself.

An unstable child puts no stock in the value of persistence. His ambition, too, does not lie in the direction of attainment even if he believes or wishes to believe that he will succeed. As his courage is limited, he gives up easily and turns to the next project. His first exaggerated enthusiasm reveals his pessimism. He cannot take his time, as he is sure that time will prove his deficiency.

There is no reason to assume that his instability is innate. Such an assumption is an excuse that the child himself has manufactured, incited perhaps by miscalculated reproofs from family and associates. Help will come only from insight into the child's scheme and an alteration of his life plan. You can talk the matter over freely with older children; but in the case of a young child the transformation can result only from your understanding of the situation. You must give him new courage and help him to change his aims. The child is not interested in *doing*, but in *getting* as much as possible with the least effort. Instead of his drive to excel or to get easy and quick results, he must discover the satisfaction which lies in work and effort, regardless of the outcome.

PASSIVE-CONSTRUCTIVE METHODS

The Clinging Vine

Children, especially when they are small, find many pleasant methods of getting attention without effort. They just have to look, and everybody stretches their hands out toward them. They adore and admire, and everybody falls for their tricks. They use their weakness and helplessness to put others in their service; but they do it so charmingly that nobody resents going out of his way to do everything for them. They never disturb or annoy, because then they would lose their power. They may tend to become scheming, and are actually completely concerned with themselves, while they appear to be interested only in others.

The tendency to lean on others sooner or later leads to disturbed relationships. As long as they can please, all is well; but when a situation does not permit pleasing, their good manners end. They may first become destructive in order to attract attention. If that fails, they may easily move into the third group of children whose exaggerated desire to be liked may lead, then, to the assumption that they are not liked at all. Many dependent children turn into hostile and even cruel beings when they find out that their charm no longer works; for instance, when they are dethroned by a new sibling.

Vanity

Children who are admired just for what they *are* and not for what they can *do* are invited to become vain. Vanity springs from the ability to attract admiration without doing anything to deserve it. Vanity is encouraged by remarks of adults who praise the child's appearance. If such recognition is considered by a child to be the basis for his social position within his family group, then his vanity becomes firmly entrenched. It is a danger of beautiful children that they learn to rely more upon their appearance and the impression they make than upon their achievements and efforts. The evolving lack of confidence in their own abilities makes them only more dependent on the approval of others and increases their vanity. This in turn eventually leads to conflict, as they demand more and contribute less.

The elimination of extreme vanity is a most difficult task. Whoever does not know that an exaggerated striving for prestige arises from strong feelings of inferiority will merely try to rebuff the seemingly vain and conceited child by disparaging him. However, this will only heighten the child's sense of inadequacy and increase the impulse toward presumptuousness or other forms of self-display. Vain children cannot bear to yield precedence to anyone, and therefore sidestep any situation in which they cannot excel. Hence, in the event of pronounced discouragement, the vain child may recoil from any activity in the presence of other people. Thus every vain child is timid whenever uncertain of success. You must learn to see through the masks of conceit—as through those of indifference. A boy may learn nothing at school, but still be ambitious. And, similarly, the complete neglect of clothes and personal appearance by no means excludes vanity. Such children have simply stopped trying to make a good impression. They are not interested in looking just neat, like all the others. If they cannot impress with their glamour, they don't care; or they may even try to impress with their sloppiness. Such "carelessness" is plainly dictated by vanity. The child would respect the conventional standards of appearance, if he were not concerned with the impression he makes.

How can we overcome vanity? Chiefly by not fostering it. Most parents stimulate vanity in the children by putting so much emphasis on "what people will say." Many parents expect the child to scintillate, either through his attractiveness or his charm. They dress him up, make a great to-do over his clothes, and rejoice in his "success." But the admiration which he receives is not sufficiently supported by his sense of his intrinsic worth. Through showing off he gives exaggerated weight to the opinions of others at the expense of his own estimation of himself. If he fails to impress, he feels his own importance questioned. But even his success does not give him real self-confidence; the ease with which he can win recognition through his external appearance often leads him to minimize productive achievements. He does not need to learn, to be industrious, to have any special abilities. Even when vanity is combined with useful and valuable activities, even then it unmistakably reveals a feeling of inadequacy. No one desires notoriety unless he believes that otherwise he is of no worth. And whoever wants to be the first will be ceaselessly tormented by the thought that sometime perhaps he may not succeed and someone else may outstrip him. Parents who require their children to be exceptional implant in them the dread of failure. The vain child is intent on making impressions only because he lives in constant fear of being unable to do so.

This apprehension—namely, the feeling that one acquires importance only through other people—is equally present in bashful and in conceited children. Both fear ridicule as the greatest of all possible misfortunes; but the vain child still has the courage to use constructive means against this danger, while the timid one desires only evasion and strives for recognition only by means of weakness and deficiency. In both instances the child must be educated to attach less importance to the opinion of others, to find his true worth in himself and his attainments. He must recognize the merit of useful contributions as contrasted with external impressions. He suffers from a false notion of human values; his ambition ought not be repressed, but directed into the proper channel.

PASSIVE-DESTRUCTIVE METHODS

Bashfulness

Ten-year-old Tess is a bashful child, just the opposite of her brother, three years younger than she. He is spirited and resolute, ready to tackle anything; she, easily embarrassed and reticent. When asked a question, she is speechless. She likes best to stay at home with her mother, and never goes out without her. At school, too, she is retiring, and has only one good friend. Very characteristic is the mother's attitude when anyone speaks to the daughter: "Why don't you answer the doctor? Don't look down at the floor! Stand up straight!" When the girl is asked a question, her mother answers for her. It is simply impossible for her to wait for the child's response. Big as the girl is, she tries to hide behind her mother's skirts. What is the meaning of this conduct?

Tess is strongly competing with her younger brother. She feels that she is slighted on his account—and not only because he is a boy. He is quicker and more vivacious, more clever and capable. The boy had been encouraged by his parents to surpass his older sister. When he was small, the girl was urged to give in to him. Everything he did was "nice" and "cute." She, who previously had been spoiled as an only child, became sulky and obstinate. She soon learned how to use her dependence and maladroitness as a means not only of evading further responsibilities in the care of her brother, but also of forcing her mother to show a greater interest in her. There was a drawback, it is true; for she had to put up with continual preaching on her awkwardness and inability. But, after all, she did succeed in concentrating her mother's attention on herself.

Many timid children follow the same scheme. (We must, however, distinguish them from those who have been cowed or, so to speak, intimidated.) Through their behavior they force other people to be concerned with them and help them. To get an answer from them takes time and effort. Their conduct is unpleasant and annoying; yet one cannot be indifferent to them. No doubt they make themselves conspicuous—by merely doing nothing. Their discouragement may be combined with ambition, otherwise these children would no longer try to get attention, but give up completely and resign themselves to complete and dull inactivity. Bashful children dread ridicule. With the aid of their timidity they strive to evade any situation in which they may have to play an active role. Still they demand and expect everybody to pay attention to them. This technique sometimes leads to serious neurotic symptoms, as, for instance, to a fear of blushing (erythrophobia). Individuals suffering from this neurosis evade all social duties, but by means of their blushing still contrive to feel that they are the object of general attention.

Tess's mother demonstrates how one should *not* treat a bashful child. The girl certainly invites constant supervision and tutelage—for this is the purpose of bashfulness. But one cannot afford to accept her invitation. The child's fear of activity and obligations can be overcome only by systematic encouragement. This process is highly complicated in the case of children who hide behind their pretended inadequacy in order to escape the requisites of living. If they are praised they either refuse to believe or are flattered, but dread all the more a future failure. It takes considerable time for such a child to regain his lost faith in himself; and it requires *systematic* work. Even encouraging and commendatory *words* are not enough. The child needs more substantial evidence of trust and recognition.

Dependence and Untidiness

Dependent children—who are often untidy—give a great deal of trouble. They always need someone to tell and remind them what to do and, finally, to *do* everything for them.

Children become dependent if forcibly deprived of their natural desire to be independent. A want of faith in the child's abilities, a desire to relieve him of inconveniences, or perhaps the parents' need to gain personal importance through their protectiveness, can lead a child to give up all desire for self-reliance. The more capable the mother, the more she tends to assign to herself all the domestic duties and responsibilities, the more likely will her child become dependent.

You should never do anything for a child that he can do for himself. If he is used to being catered to and waited on, then this procedure must be stopped. Naturally you should not be impatient. If the child is awkward from lack of practice, it will take time until he can develop skill. Meanwhile you can encourage him and spur him on, but never should you relieve him of any obligation, either from impatience or a misdirected sympathy.

It is not always the parents alone who are responsible for their child's lack of self-reliance.

Eight-year-old Trudi can do nothing for herself, or, if she does manage to finish a task, it is wretchedly done. She goes about everything the wrong way to invite constant assistance. When the family goes for a walk, she lags behind and has to be called and finally fetched. She can dress herself, but none too neatly. Even her food is cut up for her. When she pours water she usually misses the glass. She is flighty, untidy, and indolent. In short, she needs someone to look after her and play servant to her. And she has this someone! Her mother, a business woman, has little time for her; but Trudi has a sister, four years older than she, who nursemaids her abundantly. Twelve-year-old Anne is earnest, intelligent, and capable beyond her age. She manages not only her own affairs—since no adult pays any attention whatsoever to the children—but also those of her sister. And she refuses to be relieved of this additional burden. Once, when the two of them were together at a camp, Anne could not be stopped from practicing her pedagogy on her younger sister. She wanted to be around her, fretting and nagging all day long, as she was accustomed to doing at home. Thus the well-bred and diligent girl disturbed the whole atmosphere of the camp, at least as much as her ill-behaved and clumsy sister.

You can see why Trudi developed as she did. The rivalry between the two sisters led to a peculiar distribution of defensive and offensive weapons. Anne may be victorious as the more capable of the two, but more attention must be paid to Trudi. One child tries to win recognition actively, through useful accomplishments; the other passively, through ineptitude. It is not enough merely to encourage Trudi. This must be done, it is true, if better accomplishments are to be expected of her. But she will avoid accomplishments because they will deprive her of the means of holding her own with her more

capable sister. Improvement can be obtained only by influenc-
ing *both* children. Their strong rivalry must be toned down;
only then would it be possible to reduce the A.G.M. on both
sides. They must learn to work *with*, not against each other.
For both are wanting in social interest. (It is characteristic,
and very understandable, that Anne, too, is unsuccessful in her
relations with other people. She has no real friends, since they
refuse her the superior position that she desires.) Thus, both
must learn to play their proper roles in life.

It is not always necessary, however, to transform the whole
life plan in order to break the child of a single undesirable
trait. A certain sense of order can be instilled in any child. The
only requisite is that we allow no carelessness. The human
organism is by nature attuned to regularity and system. Un-
tidiness is first developed as a trick or device. The child recognizes the advantage of not getting up on time, failing to wash
and dress himself, being late for meals, refusing to put away
his toys, or not going to bed at the set hour. In these ways
he wins his victories in his struggle with mother and father,
and thus secures the attention that he wishes. In order to wean
him away from such habits, it is necessary to avoid conflict
and bring the natural consequences to bear. But parents
themselves must observe order, or else the child will soon use
their own failing against them.

Lack of Concentration and Stamina

A child's incapacity for work is often blamed on a supposed
mental or physical weakness that keeps him from paying sus-
tained attention to a task for any period of time. This assumption of a "lack of energy," of an impairment of "nervous
energy," is utterly erroneous, though it may seem to be confirmed by the experiences of anxious parents and timorous
individuals. Such people tend to attribute their own failures,
or those of their children, to nervous debility or some other
constitutional weakness. This, like the ready assumption of

congenital feeble-mindedness in each case of seeming stupidity, leads in turn to an aggravation of the complaints.

Fifteen-year-old Fran is a nervous, "weak" child. She is attending high school and has much difficulty, although she is bright. She tires so easily that after school she often spends the remainder of the day in bed. It is even hard for her to pay attention in class. And when she has some unusual assignment, or faces the prospect of an examination, she goes completely to pieces. The night before, she cannot eat or sleep. Sometimes she gets so ill that she has to stay in bed when she should be taking a test. Even in elementary school she could not bear to sit quietly and hold her hands still. In her earlier years she had to repeat a grade, and for this reason it was at first decided not to send her to high school, but, by weeping and wheedling, she succeeded in getting her way, since all her friends were attending. However, she keeps up with her work only with the greatest difficulty and she needs continual help.

Parents and doctors assumed a constitutional weakness. But what was the real cause of this condition? Until she was four, Fran was well developed, energetic and lively. But at this age she changed completely. She is an only child. Her mother lived on very bad terms with her father, and devoted little time to the child, whom she left to a nursemaid; but still she was very ambitious for Fran. The girl was never pretty enough to suit her. She bought her the most attractive clothes and dressed her like a princess. Fran set great store by her appearance. She would cry and pout for a day if she got a pair of shoes that failed to please her. She was generally pitied because her father treated her and her mother so badly and eventually deserted them. Her relatives bought her whatever she desired. When she passed a shop window and saw something she liked, she stopped and cried until she got it.

Yet on the whole she was very well behaved, and never *directly* imposed her will on others. She had different means of getting what she wanted. Until she was ten the maid had to dress and undress her. She was very compliant, and by accommodating herself to everyone she succeeded wonderfully in making everyone her servant. Today she still plays the "cute little girl" and runs about in socks and hairbows. No one is hardhearted enough to refuse her anything. She always selects either older children or very young ones as playmates. And even the younger girls immediately mother her, which she graciously permits. But she much prefers to play with grown-ups. Her mother dissuaded her from becoming intimate with other girls, claiming that they would only teach her bad habits. Hence she likes best of all to play alone.

From her fourth year on, she used her weakness systematically as a means to get service. She had to be urged to eat—and promptly lost weight. She became exhausted on long walks. Once, in the country, when she was so big that her relatives could no longer carry her, they had to hire a man to transport her home! She could not do housework; everything was too hard for her, and she always steered clear of the kitchen. She was never apt at handiwork—she tired too quickly. She always wanted to make something for her mother, but could never get it done.

Fran's mother paid no attention to her unless she was ill. And in the last few years she became ill very often. An impending test at school, as we have seen, was enough to send her off to bed. To what extent her good behavior is only a show and a means of making an impression can be seen from the following detail. The desk and shelves in her room are littered with schoolbooks—and a hodgepodge of other books. She never reads them, except when somebody enters the room; then she seems deeply engrossed in some lesson or self-set task that she will never complete.

Here you can plainly recognize the devices employed by an ambitious child who finds it hard to win recognition by useful accomplishments. Fran's boundless ambition is surely obvious, though no one around her suspects it since she never attempted any real achievements at school or elsewhere, but strove to avoid them. Her seeming "constitutional weakness" proved to be her most effective alibi; and, what is more, it also served to support her in her demands for being nursed and mothered.

Like Fran, many children try to take refuge behind frailty and use it as a means of making their parents their slaves. Then they are exempt from responsibilities out of consideration for this "weakness." Yet if you try to *force* them to conformity, you will soon find out that this weakness is stronger than your strength. No violence or pressure can move the child to co-operate. His ambition, the whole trend of his endeavors, must be turned in a new direction. The previous pampering must be superseded by a systematic program of joint *work*. Hitherto the child has been the *object* of solicitude, and he has taken full advantage of this fact. Now he has to become a fellow worker.

Self-indulgence and Frivolity

Fifteen-year-old George is a flighty, unrestrained boy who lives only for the moment. He is an only child, who, in his first year, was entrusted to an aunt because his parents had no time to care for him. This aunt had a daughter three years older than George, but favored the boy in order to make him forget the lack of his own home. He always got a bigger helping of pudding and more than his share of candy. Later he had more pocket money, and was allowed to sleep longer than her own daughter. She was given only bread and butter for her school lunch, while George always had meat in his sandwiches. Only George was helped with his homework. Until he was eight, his aunt washed him, while her daughter had to wash herself when she was little more than a baby.

Despite this preferential treatment there was no open conflict between the two children. The girl adjusted herself to the situation; a certain independence and capability compensated her for the neglect that she experienced. She tried to mother George, too, for he had by now developed a peculiar faculty. He was an attractive child, and knew how to ingratiate himself (passive-constructive A.G.M.). No one could resist him. He exploited to the limits all the persons with whom he came in contact, and had a charming way of "pumping" relatives and acquaintances for money, which he promptly spent on candy. At school, too, he crept into the favor of his teacher, and became her acknowledged pet. He got into a great deal of mischief, but no one could stay angry with him, and his pranks were always forgiven. When he entered high school he encountered his first real reversal. His usual methods were ineffective. Honest work was required and he was unprepared. At elementary school he had made a straight record of A's; he barely passed the first grade of high school. At this time he shifted from passive-constructive methods to passive-destructive behavior.

It is obvious that George's whole personality was conditioned by his childhood situation and the way in which he tried to master it. There would be no value in singling out his frivolity and greediness and making them the subject of a campaign to reform him. He is very ambitious but his aspiration is *to get as much as possible out of other people*. Only when he succeeds in this does he feel important. Work is burdensome to him. He has no desire to control himself because then he would have to relinquish his demands upon others and upon life. He has not discovered the joy of active achievement. Success through accomplishment presupposes a long period of exertion, and this is something that George has never tried. He does not plan for the future; he wants everything *immediately*. Hence he cannot stand tension or suspense, but uses these as a means of securing greater momentary advantages. He runs away from home if anything chances to displease him, and incurs debts from friends when his family refuses him the money he wants. Through his insidious helplessness he makes other people reap what *he* has sown. With his lack of restraint or discipline he extorts whatever he wishes.

The greatest obstacle to diverting George from his course is his relatives. His readjustment depends upon whether they can be induced to adopt a more reasonable attitude. When an attempt was made to put him into a foster home he ran away and was promptly reaccepted by his family. Thereupon he made life miserable for everybody; there was no one to make him bear the consequences when he brazenly flouted the established order. And yet this is the only means of finally opening his eyes. From the attitude of his environment George must naturally conclude that he has found the right methods for asserting himself. And, if his family cannot bring themselves to stop yielding to his wishes, they will begin a desperate struggle, with threats, affronts, abasements, and coercion, which in turn will only increase his resistance and his rebellion against order. He no longer seeks merely attention and service, but power and perhaps even revenge.

Steadfastness on the part of the family, and a continued process of encouraging George—these are the methods that may mark the way to a transformation of his life plan.

Greediness characterizes persons who aim at cheap momentary success because they have little confidence in the future. Whatever they cannot get at the moment seems to them highly uncertain of attainment. This lack of faith in the future is typical of greedy children. They are unable to save. Why should they? Tomorrow will be unpleasant enough without ruining today. Hence it is of no consequence to them that today's enjoyment brings tomorrow's discomfort. They take this as part of the bargain. They are children who feel threatened by more successful brothers and sisters or are pampered by inconsistent parents. Naturally a certain amount of defiance is involved when the child tries, against all orders, to obtain "treats." The candy bought on the sly, the jam pilfered from the pantry, the chocolate bars consumed at one sitting that should have lasted a week—these not only taste good, but signify easy triumphs over the adults, without requiring work and effort. Greediness and discouragement are always closely associated. Thus the greediness of a child shows that his psychic equilibrium is upset and that he needs help. But once again: help is not synonymous with indulgence.

Anxiety and Fear

In the earlier discussion of extreme conscientiousness we mentioned the problem of neurosis. At the center of all neurotic phenomena is fear. But whereas deep fear in the adult is considered pathological, fear in children is considered natural. It appears occasionally in every child. Only when it becomes severe is it regarded as unusual.

Fear is the expression of helplessness. Whoever feels that he is weak dreads not only real, imminent dangers; his anxiety seeks out vague and unknown menaces. In man, and perhaps in all living beings, the fear reactions are the innate recollections of a more primitive mode of life; for the aboriginal peoples are actually under constant threat of dangers, some of which are unknown, others incomprehensible to the primitive mind. Civilized man, under normal conditions, lives sheltered within his social community. But still the child feels his helplessness, and this feeling takes form in his susceptibility to fear; and as we sympathize with his helplessness, we respond to his fear.

Here is the crux of the problem. The child learns *to use his innate fear reactions to achieve his personal goals*. The more impressed the parents are by the child's anxiety (whether from excessive love, from sympathy, or because they suffer from their own fears), the more readily they succumb to his scheme of action. Through fear, the child may make himself a tyrant who lives beyond the pale of all order and system.

A timid child dreads solitude and darkness, and through his fear reveals his characteristic weakness and its cause. Only a spoiled child will react in this way. He thinks it the worst of all fates to be left alone, because he feels incapable of existing without the aid of adults. Nothing is more terrifying than to be alone, for then he has to depend entirely on himself. And, similarly, in the darkness he is completely dependent upon his own resources. Sometimes the parents themselves provide the child with arguments that he can use against them; they resort to solitude as a punishment or use the spectral "bogyman" or ill suited fairy-tales to paint the horrors of darkness and night. The typical childhood fear is often developed through the child's refusal to go to bed. Many children object to being sent to bed; either they are unwilling to give up, even temporarily, the warmth and solicitude of their parents, or they resent the slight implied in not being allowed to stay up as late as the grown-ups or older brothers and sisters. Hence going to bed, with the correlated necessity of staying alone in the dark, becomes a subject of resentment. And in this case fear proves itself to be a weapon that few parents can resist.

The degree of dependency to which parents can be brought by this device is often absurd. The child will not go to bed alone. The door must be kept open, or there has to be at least a slit to admit the light that symbolizes contact with others. Gradually the requirements may increase: the door to the adjoining room must remain open; a lamp must be left burning; a grown-up must stay in the room until the child falls asleep; the mother must sit by his bed and hold his hand; if she lets go, he immediately sets up a howl; even after he has fallen asleep, he senses his mother's attempted withdrawal, wakes up, cries, and keeps her at his bedside until deep in the night. Children who have accepted the necessity of going to sleep by themselves may still find it possible, through nightmares and nocturnal spells of fright, to creep into the parents' bed and escape the dreaded solitude.

In the daytime, too, fear proves itself effectual.

Twelve-year-old Paul uses his fearfulness to dominate his entire family. He is a late-born child, with two adult siblings. Everyone pampers and indulges him; but he lives in constant anxiety. At night the door must be kept open. In the evening he cannot stay alone in a room. He evades every situation in which he would be left to himself. He dreads schoolwork, is afraid when the other boys fight, cannot swim or participate in gymnastics. Whenever his mother attempts to leave, violent scenes follow. And so his family always tries to comfort him, to help him, and to smooth the way for him.

His mother came to consult me, but not because of concern about the child's anxiety. She asked for a certificate excusing him from swimming class—the poor boy could never sleep the night before! That he might learn to stand on his own feet, trust in his own strength, and cope with his own difficulties—this was a possibility that had never entered her mind. And never would Paul have attempted it of his own accord; for he likes the sheltered atmosphere he lives in, though he pays for it dearly with his fears.

Paul, however, is still rather conservative in his choice of methods.

Fourteen-year-old Ernest has done a better job of training his parents. They must tell to the minute when he can expect them home, for the suspense is unendurable. He conceals his imperious egotism behind a much-stressed love for his parents. He lives under the incessant fear that something might happen *to them.* And that is why he insists on punctuality. If they stay out longer than they indicated, they must phone at regular intervals to assure him of their continued well-being. And no one realizes that what Ernest wants is to make his parents show attention to him.

What steps can be taken against the exaggerated fears of children? Force, naturally, is useless. The best course to follow is to *ignore anxiety.* The child naturally will fight this policy by every means, and stir himself up to all sorts of "states." While he is still small, he can simply be allowed to spend his fury and quiet down. You must give him the affection, love, and concern which he wants and needs, but not under the pressure of his fear. In difficult cases it may be necessary to call in a pediatrician or a psychiatrist.[1] Sometimes, too, it is possible to succeed in obviating anxiety by stimulating the child's ambition and sense of pride—by representing fear as a natural device of little children which is beneath his dignity to employ. Above all, you should not focus your attention on the *symptom*, but seek the deeper *causes*.

The child's helplessness usually springs from his sense of dependence upon adults. Accordingly, he must be granted the opportunity to acquire a greater degree of self-reliance. The observant parent will see that the anxiety becomes more pronounced when the child is faced by a problem. Hence he must learn to contend with difficult situations. *And here the parent's anxiety is more dangerous than his own.* Also his tendency to make himself the center and get his own way at any price must be corrected. Less indulgence is the best means to this end, as has been repeatedly stressed. The fact that the child's anxiety is based on undue indulgence becomes obvious, as he loses his

<hr />

[1] See opening pages of Part II.

fears completely in strange surroundings where no indulgence is shown him. Yet severity can only heighten his sense of helplessness. In this case the necessity to repress his fears may lead to deeper disturbances, usually of a neurotic nature.

Eating Difficulties

No child will become a feeding problem if his parents do not try to make him eat. Eating difficulties begin when mother or father attaches an inordinate importance to the child's eating. This may occur very early if the mother is overanxious about his weight, or if the child is sickly or has lost weight during illness. Then he is exposed to a pressure which at first may be only mild but eventually may develop into force and finally into violent coercion. Being urged to eat disturbs one's ability and willingness to accept food. It upsets the normal functioning of the stomach and makes eating repulsive. Furthermore, a child exposed to pressure reacts in general with resistance. If this resistance is directed against the intake of food, the parents, already overconcerned with the eating procedure, increase their pressure. Their desperation may grow by leaps and bounds, but will never improve the child's feeding. Moreover, it gives the child the impression that eating is not for his own interest, but for his parents' sake. Thus eating becomes a ready weapon to be used against them, especially if the child feels neglected or slighted. Such may be the case if a new baby arrives, or if the child has recovered from an illness and the parents stop their special attention.

A two-year-old girl resisted any food offered to an extent that worried not only her mother but the family physician. The child developed tantrums at each meal, and went for days without food if left on her own. It was possible to trace the beginning of this aversion to food to its origin. The mother was advised to keep the child on regular feeding hours (which was good advice), but what methods did she use? When the child was asleep at the hour of feeding she awakened her. When the child refused to take the bottle, she did not—as she should have done—let the child go until the next feeding time; instead, she forced the bottle into her mouth. When the child refused to take her first spoonful of fruit juice the mother took an even more drastic step; she held the child's nose, waiting until the child opened her mouth to breathe, and then put the spoon into the gasping mouth. Is it any wonder that this child developed such an antagonism against food?

All eating difficulties vanish within a few days or weeks if parents permit the child's natural impulses to exert themselves. These impulses are present *in every child*. Let him go hungry, and after a while he will ask for food. If you provide this food at regular times he will automatically adjust himself.

Instead of following this simple procedure, parents who have difficulties with their children's eating habits behave generally in a way which would make every normal child a food problem. First, they try persuasion. Mealtime becomes a tragic farce. The mother warns the child of the dire consequences if he does not eat. She feeds him and coaxes. She tells stories or gives good advice. She offers rewards or threatens punishment. Eventually she becomes angry; she begins to scold or to shout and even uses violence in stuffing the food into the child's mouth. Such a mother can become a fury out of sheer love, never noticing how the child twists and writhes until he finally throws up the food so laboriously forced into him. Now she either gives in and lets him go without food or she prepares special foods according to his preference. There are mothers who spend a large portion of each day planning a menu that the child will like and accept. Or the mother becomes determined and decides—"just to get him used to it"— to give him the same food at the next meal that he refused at the last, naturally with the same results. And yet, both parents and child could so easily be spared these agonies.

In the first place, the child's eating is no subject for discussion and no reason for commotion. Parents should trust the child's healthy instincts. He will not starve if you refrain from meddling, which only serves to stifle his instincts. With your concern you provide him a satisfaction much greater than his physical satiation. Think of all the attention he gets from you! He is even in a position to overpower you, to render you completely helpless, just by not eating. These social gains are more desirable than physical comfort. No child, left to his own resources in the midst of plenty, could develop malnutrition and dietary deficiencies to such a degree as children frequently show whose parents worry about their physical development and force them to eat. The first step in correcting a child's eating habits is to let him alone. No word should be spoken, no comment be made about finishing his plate or hurrying. But it is not enough to keep quiet. An anxious mother can speak eloquently without opening her mouth. If you sit at the table staring at the child, expressing all your tension, apprehension, despair, and fury, you give him just as much undue attention and provoke his defiance.

Secondly, the child must experience the natural consequences of his refusal to eat. If he does not want to eat what is set before him he should be granted the privilege of rejecting the food. But you should not indulge him and, out of pity or fear, give him something else to eat. When he does not eat his meal he must wait for food until the next meal—no snacks, no candy or bread and butter, not even a glass of milk outside of the set routine. And at the next meal he should be given the same food that the rest of the family is served.

Pampered children may "condescend" to eat those dishes that "taste good." If they get away with such demands, the parents either do not understand the importance of order or are helpless to stop their overindulgence. It is most important that the child learn to eat everything. It is not difficult to induce a child to eat even food that he dislikes, unless his aversion is based on organic sensitivity (allergy). If he does not finish his serving with the rest of the family, the plate should be removed and he should be given nothing more during this meal. If you wish to train him to eat a certain food, you can arrange to follow it with his favorite dessert. He should know what is coming, but you must be careful to mention it in a way that is neither a reward nor a punishment. Such threats as "If you don't eat your spinach, you won't get your ice cream" are entirely out of place. A casual attitude is imperative. But you must be firm and resist all promises, temper tantrums, or other tricks with which he may try to impress and weaken you. You must express your sympathy with him but must not give in. You should not be impressed even when he strives hard to eat what does not appeal to him but cannot get it down. As soon as he gags and struggles with his food, you just remove his plate and tell him that apparently he is not hungry and that he should not force himself; but the consequences must take place just the same.

Little Fred was invited to a party. Apparently he was a very poor eater. All the rest of the children had finished, but Fred still had almost his whole cup of cocoa and chewed away on a sandwich without noticeable effect. His grandmother who was with him remarked that it often took him an hour to finish his milk. She tried to persuade him. "Aren't you ashamed, Fred? All the others have almost finished; hurry up." The hostess asked her to leave the room and then turned to the boy. "At our house you don't have to eat if you don't want to. Give me your cup and your sandwich." And she made a gesture of taking them away. At once Fred grabbed them with both hands and took a huge bite of the sandwich. Now he had both cheeks full, but he could not get the food down. His training was against him. So she persisted. "No, Fred, that won't do. I can tell you are not hungry, so I will just have to take the food away from you if you don't want to eat it." Nothing more was said. In five minutes the cocoa was gone and the sandwich consumed, to the great amazement of the grandmother who could not understand how the feat had been accomplished.

Another case—and one of the worst in my experience—was that of little John. He was seven years old when his mother brought him to my summer camp. He had just recovered from whooping cough. He coughed and vomited not only when he started to eat, but also whenever he became excited or exerted himself physically. He had lost so much weight that he was down to skin and bones. The frantic parents had hired a nurse who fed him several times during the day. Each feeding took hours. The nurse had literally to force each bite into his mouth. The result was that a small amount of food did get eaten, but most of the time it did not stay down.

I was willing to accept the boy on the condition that the parents would not visit him for two weeks and would not inquire about his gain or loss of weight. The parents had already tried everything else; they had no alternative. The boy ate actually nothing for a few days. When food was placed before him he just looked at it. Nobody made any remarks; after a little while the plate was removed and, according to the rules, nothing else was offered to him. He took only milk and fluids at the time when they were served to all children. It was difficult to watch this child starve himself without doing something about it—but it was the only way to cure him.

Toward the end of the first week, John started to put some food into his mouth. The way in which he did it may best be described in the following anecdote: We had taken an excursion into the surrounding mountains. I encountered John on top of a hill and asked him how he was. He did not answer. This was puzzling as he was generally very friendly and conforming. I tried to find out what was troubling him but was unable to get any response. Finally I asked him to open his mouth. He obliged. There was his roll which he had taken at breakfast, one hour ago. He had put it in his mouth but had neither chewed nor swallowed it. It took two weeks of patient waiting before he started to eat normally. But then all difficulties were gone and he picked up weight very rapidly.

I observed another characteristic episode in a summer camp. A boy of fourteen had suffered from some abdominal tumor and had undergone several operations during the past few years. At the time he was physically well but could not eat. He vomited as soon as he took food. He was extremely underweight and in danger of starvation.

On this first day in camp, at dinnertime, he did not like the soup which was served. It was explained to him that he did not have to eat but he would not get anything else for this meal. Still he refused to eat. Then, when the meat was served he "became hungry" but he was not given anything. He said in amazement, "But I want to eat!" Apparently he had never experienced refusal when he was ready to eat. He was told in a friendly but firm manner that he had our sympathy, but that the rule could not be broken. At this point some other children intervened. They saw how undernourished he was, and when he started to cry, they begged that he be given some food. Everybody felt badly about it. But giving in to him would have meant losing the battle. He did not get anything on this day, but after a few days he ate everything and his vomiting stopped. This verified the diagnosis of the consulting physician, that the eating difficulties and the vomiting were of a psychogenic nature and probably the result of the overconcern and coaxing of his parents whose apprehensions and fear were only too understandable.

Speech Impediments

Occasional slight speech disturbances occur normally during the child's development and should not be regarded as pathological. So-called natural stuttering may, however, lead to more serious disorders when the parents intervene with warning, admonishments, and reproaches. Thus speech, too, may become the core of a conflict in which the child wins his victories against all parental efforts. Stuttering is directed specifically against contact with people; it impairs association with others. The child demands special assurance for making contacts. Stuttering often appears in the presence of persons whom the child fears. Sometimes, however, excessive ambition lies at its roots. The child does not so much fear the people themselves as he fears the possibility of disgracing himself. Stuttering is a symptom of anxiety and of fear of failure; but at the same time it signifies opposition, producing concern and special attention.

Stuttering may require professional treatment, yet the problem is less one of speech exercises than of general readjustment. Parents can help by not paying attention to the disturbance and—what is still more important—by applying all possible methods to reduce his antagonism and lessen his feeling of inadequacy.

One particular speech disturbance definitely results from extreme indulgence and pampering. This is a kind of pseudo-muteness. The child acts like a deaf mute without being one. Sometimes it is difficult to determine whether he is actually a deaf mute or not. He never talks or listens. He does not find it necessary to say anything, since his family grants all his wishes, which he indicates with gestures and facial expressions. Appropriate treatment *of the parents* always leads to the removal of the muteness, thereby permitting a final diagnosis.

Similar mechanisms produce inadequate speech in smaller children. They talk very indistinctly so that nobody except the members of the family can understand them. Their lack of participation in communicating with others is in line with a general "laziness." Such children make no proper efforts in any direction. They successfully demand that others do everything necessary. They walk slowly, dragging their feet; they do not dress themselves and have to be fed—all similar devices for getting attention in a passive-destructive way. They may seem dull and apathetic but actually they are clever enough to realize that they need not do more, as everything is done for them. Why should they exert themselves unnecessarily if they get so much comforting attention by doing nothing? If one succeeds in restraining an overprotective mother—or an older sister who gains status by her management of the "baby"—the "baby" soon grows up and assumes all the activities which he refused even when exposed to violent force.

Inarticulate speech is only one symptom of artificial babyhood. If you wish to improve the child's pronunciation, you should ignore whatever he says if it is not clearly expressed.

It is inadvisable to correct his pronunciation or to get him to **repeat** a word correctly. All this is undue attention which will stimulate the child to continue his defects rather than to give them up. He will improve his speech only when he finds it beneficial to himself to do so. The advantage of speaking correctly will appear if he is unable to make himself understood otherwise.

CHAPTER 2

Striving for Power

Whenever the child's efforts to gain social status by attracting attention fail, a new phase of social relationships begins.
In most instances, it becomes a struggle for power. By being
able to do what he is not supposed to do and refusing to do
what is required of him, the child challenges your power and
tries to make himself a potent force within the group. The
idea of power is, of course, not the child's invention. He realizes from his observation of parents, relatives, and acquaintances that power gives social status and settles issues. Whoever
can overpower the others gains triumph, is considered smart
and superior. The whole atmosphere of our contemporary
family, as part of our society, favors the mutual struggle for
dominance and power. When other methods of trying to be a
part of the social group fail, the contest for power looms as
the next attempt for social recognition.

DISOBEDIENCE

Disobedience is a characteristic tool of the child's struggle
for power. This struggle disturbs cooperation and the necessary order. Whenever the question of power arises, the child
stops conforming. Thus, disobedience is the most frequent and
universal expression of the child's revolt. It occurs in conjunc-
tion with a great variety of other "faults." It must be remem-
bered, however, that every healthy child offers occasional
resistance. Children who always obey implicitly are not well-
bred, but cowed children. In their case, resistance does not
come out into the open; their faults are of a different nature.

A child is not disobedient merely because he does not do everything exactly as he should. It is when you need to enforce order that the child reveals the extent of his reluctance to obey. Some children do the opposite of what they are asked to do, as a matter of principle.

Six-year-old Jack is a great trial to his mother. When he is supposed to be dressing he runs around naked, and at mealtime he refuses to leave his toys. He pays no attention if asked to do something, and when told to come into the room he is bound to go in the opposite direction. His mother is completely nonplussed.

Jack is an only child. His father is a "weak" person who makes the mother's life miserable by his nervous complaints. She is a diligent, capable woman, but even she cannot stand the nervousness of her husband. In the end she always gives in to him, and maintains household discipline only through great effort on her part. Her attempts to instill orderly habits in Jack meet with violent opposition from her husband, who is extremely attached to the child and wants to relieve him of every inconvenience. He always takes the boy's part against the mother. If the little fellow expresses any wish, his father grants it at once, regardless of the mother's objections; and Jack has learned to take advantage of this situation. He does whatever he wants to do, for he is under his father's protection; and whenever his mother tries to insist, he immediately takes refuge with the father. The mother feels that she should counterbalance her husband's indulgence with severity, but this serves only to increase the child's resistance.

The life plan of this boy can be understood from his position between two warring despots. By allying himself with the one and defying the other he strives to win his position in the family. He knows no other triumphs than those over his mother's authority. His ideal is not ability and personal worth, but victory through resistance. And he turns on this potent disobedience as often as opportunity permits. Even when his mother asks him to do something that he might like to do under other conditions, he will do precisely the opposite. His fundamental error is his belief that defiance alone can secure power and prestige. He is far behind in useful accomplishments. He can dress himself only with difficulty; he is disorderly and lacks self-reliance; and he frequently stutters.

The greatest parental deficiency is naturally the incredible indulgence of the father, although the mother's efficiency may play a part in the deficiency of both her husband and her son. Disobedience often occurs in connection with spoiling, for an act of disobedience presupposes an inexcusable compliance on the part of the parent. Undoubtedly mother spoils and over-protects Jack, too—perhaps out of consideration for the ailing father and his excitability, or perhaps because she likes to take on too much responsibility. In any event, the boy has never yet experienced his mother's ability to enforce her wishes. Instead of attempting enforcement, she gives new orders: "Jack, do this, go there, let that alone!" And when Jack shows not the slightest inclination to obey these commands, she repeats them. As this does not help, the mother begins to scream at the boy, or she slaps him. Finally, she lets him have his own way since she does not want to bother with him any longer.

This attitude on the mother's part is characteristic of the development of disobedience. We can observe it again in a similar case.

Fred is a willful boy of eight. His mother died when he was quite young, and he has been living with his grandmother. The household includes several uncles and aunts and a sister who is almost ten years older than he. He is always getting into mischief, and is a typical "enfant terrible," the perfect "brat." Never under any circumstances does he behave. He is always fidgeting or prowling about; he never sits still for any length of time. He invariably has something in his hand, usually some breakable object that he will eventually drop on the floor with a resounding crash. Day in, day out, he is admonished, "Fred, hold your legs straight, don't drum with your fingers, let the bowl alone, stay in your chair!" The whole family takes part in this edifying chorus of remonstrance. But Fred ignores them. Only when the shouts become deafening or when he is slapped will he stop one nuisance—merely to begin another. No one knows what to do with him. At school he behaves in the same way. He is fidgety, always chattering and disturbing the class. He writes a wretched hand, and spells accordingly. Yet he is an intelligent, bright boy, who often so disarms you with his responses and remarks that you have to laugh—and let him do as he pleases.

What is this boy's life plan, and how did it originate? He is the youngest and smallest in a family of adults. His sister, the only other sibling, is already quite grown up and was always his superior in ability, inasmuch as she promptly took over the functions of the deceased mother and became very capable. Ever since his mother's death, Fred has felt sorry for himself, although all his relatives, out of pity and because of his lovableness, pampered him greatly and gave in to him in everything. Quite early he must have come to the conclusion that he could assert himself in this family group only by making the others concern themselves with him. He was unable to see any other way of confirming his importance. So he became dependent and failed in his schoolwork. By these means, and especially by his trick of making himself conspicuous, he compelled the others to pay constant attention to him. As they became increasingly annoyed and attempted to subdue him, Fred's A.G.M. turned into a struggle for power.

By now it should be clear that any attempt to rear Fred properly is doomed to failure unless we succeed first in changing his opinion of himself. He believes that he is of no importance, and that there is no other way of holding his ground than by making a spectacle of himself, attracting everyone's attention, and having his own way. If we want to help the boy, we must make him see that he, too, can win recognition and esteem through useful contributions. It will not be easy to impress the value of real achievements on the mind of a child who is so terribly discouraged; but such encouragement is essential. Above all, we shall have to show an interest in him in those rare instances when he is not in mischief and when he really contributes something. The alteration of the life style is the most important premise of improvement. Disobedience in particular remains unintelligible unless we know and understand the *entire background* of the child's conflict.

In addition to spoiling, certain purely technical errors in

training play a part in the development of disobedience. We shall briefly recapitulate here a few of those that have previously been mentioned: inconsistency in giving orders; indecisiveness of tone; violent, offensive or humiliating approaches and expressions; and impatience that does not even wait for the execution of a command. The most drastic error, however, consists in the repetition of an order. Every command with which the child does not comply increases his general disobedience. It is necessary to give specific commands only very rarely, when compliance is absolutely essential. But when something has been said *once*, it must not be repeated a second time; for the *words* are of no avail, and *actions* must take their place. It is self-evident that these should not consist in the application of *force*. Whenever the child does not respond to an order, you can and must allow the natural consequence of his behavior to take full effect.

This can be done quite peaceably. Especially in the case of a very willful child must you delay a command until the proper time arrives—a time when you are prepared to answer nonresponse with a logical consequence. Such occasions are more frequent than parents who evade reflection can imagine. In any event you must avoid the heaping up of commands and injunctions. The child must first of all learn to mind. If he has found in two or three instances that you are in a position to enforce your orders, he will be more apt to heed your words.

A youngster of two or three is standing in front of a display window and refuses to budge. His mother and father have gone ahead and are shouting at him and coaxing him. But the boy refuses to leave the spot. The parents are desperate. The father comes back and speaks loudly and sharply. The child pretends not to hear. Finally the father's patience is exhausted. He grasps the boy and begins to drag him off. And now the real show begins. The child resists fiercely; he howls and screams and throws himself on the sidewalk. Mother and father tug away at him in great excitement. A crowd gathers and takes sides with or against the parents, until the father picks the boy up bodily and retires with him from the battlefield, not at all a radiant victor.

And yet it is so easy to bring a child like this to his senses! There is no need for uproar and turmoil. If the parents had been wise they would have told the child after his first refusal to move on, "You want to see the display window, do you? Well, we're sorry but we haven't the time, so you'll have to stay by yourself and we'll be going on home." And if the boy had seen that they were really in earnest and were actually leaving, he hardly would have failed to follow. But suppose that he has previously been treated so laxly that he does not take his parents seriously and is convinced that now as always they will give in to him. In this event they need only turn the next corner and cautiously watch him from their vantage point. When they have disappeared, he will probably trot after them.

There are situations in which it is not easy to find the logical consequences. First of all, the time of company is not the proper time for training. (But on the other hand, you must not, from dread of a row, let the child have a free hand, or else he will take advantage of your fear of embarrassment.) When the proper time arrives, you can give the restless child the choice of sitting quietly or remaining alone in the room, since you simply cannot stand his company under such conditions. Similarly, when he fails to be quiet at mealtimes and does not conduct himself properly, there is no choice but for him to eat alone, either at a little table of his own, since he is still unable to act grown up, or perhaps even in the kitchen where he can eat as he chooses. It can be seen that it is unnecessary to exhort and command and run the risk of having him do as he pleases after all. But you should never *threaten* with consequences, only *apply* them!

In the case of unruly *older* children it is sometimes very difficult to see that an order is carried out without using brute force. Here it is best to introduce negative consequences. Refusal to submit can be maintained against even the strongest boy. If he does not arrive punctually for meals, all his violence cannot succeed in getting him a special serving. If mother leaves the room, he cannot prevent her from doing so. If he follows, she can leave the house. It would, of course, be a mistake to try to send *him* out of the room if he refuses to behave suitably. This could not be done without force, and probably not even then. Much depends, therefore, on how you construct the situation from which a child is to learn obedience.

Since the child's disobedience indicates rebellion and defiance, the hostile atmosphere must be cleared before the fault can be repaired. In the case of Jack we have clearly seen the serious error that the mother committed. She made scarcely any effort at all to win the boy over. Naturally it was no easy task to compete with the fawning indulgence of her husband. But she could certainly have found ways of interesting the child and gaining his confidence if she had not felt constrained to compensate the father's weakness with special severity on her part. Hence, when a child refuses to mind, you must first avoid arousing a conflict. Instead, you should devote more time and attention to the child in moments when he is in a good frame of mind and ready for friendly cooperation. By this means you will succeed best in obstructing the sources of his resistance.

STUBBORNNESS

Stubbornness is a variety of disobedience. Hence much that was said in the previous section is equally true here. What should be your attitude toward the child when he has a spell of stubbornness? Persuasion, threats, and promises, even the application of force, are usually futile. The child sulks and refuses to be moved.

Twelve-year-old Joe has occasional attacks of stubbornness. Sunday the family had planned to go to a restaurant for dinner, but instead they were invited to the home of some friends. Joe was furious. When they arrived, he stayed outside in the yard and could not be persuaded to go into the house. The parents sent his older brother out to fetch him, and the children of the house did their bit to convince him; but all efforts were wasted. Joe later told me how much it pleased him to have everybody entreating him—it was worth missing the dinner. But his fury really started when they finally gave up urging him and went back inside. Then at last he began to regret his mulishness.

Life had been no bed of roses for Joe. He was completely overshadowed by his elder brother. In his own opinion, nothing useful and worth while that he could do could compare with the attainments of this brother, whose superiority was constantly impressed upon Joe. Solely through his frequent attacks of stubbornness could he make himself the absolute master of his family, who were at a loss to know what to do with him. In these moments even the brother was insignificant, and he, Joe, became the hub and axis of the household.

Obstinate children use their behavior as a means of provoking people to fight with them. And most parents fall neatly into the trap. Stubbornness is one of the many devices by which children who feel abused or neglected try to attract attention and to demonstrate their strength. ("You can't make me do it!") The best answer, therefore, is to *leave the child to himself.* You can gradually break him of using these tactics if you take pains to understand his conflicts and relieve his anger by improving your relationship with him.

TEMPER TANTRUMS

Intensely combative and hostile emotions may create symptoms that appear almost pathological. Yet behind them is nothing but the desire for power and ascendancy. This is true of fits of temper. Some parents may assume an organic affection of the nerves, a nervous debility or a hereditary defect. Temper, however, is always curable through proper treatment; but parents who are afraid that a nervous disposition is the cause of temper give in to the child at the crucial moment.

You may be easily inclined to such an attitude if you or some other member of the family likewise suffers from a violent temper. In this event the assumption of an inherited predisposition becomes a foregone conclusion. Yet this person (let us assume he is the father) may also be a discouraged individual who feels an occasional urge to play the tyrant. Through the impressive spectacle of uncurbed violence he tries to prove that he cannot be tampered with. And if he seems to regret his conduct afterward, he is only masking his intentions from himself and others by his contrition and self-reproach. The whole family comes to respect his "weak nerves" and recognizes that in such moments all their own rights and prerogatives must be suspended. If the child observes outbursts of temper in his father, he may try similar expedients to compensate for a weak position; and he is encouraged to proceed in this direction when the other members of the family, horrified at his morbid "heritage," give in to his fits just as they do to his father's.

The mother of a four-year-old boy had a great deal of trouble with his fits of temper. She was firmly convinced that he had inherited this "affliction" from his father. The child was born after his father's death; hence he could not have acquired the trait by imitation. A more thorough inquiry into the circumstances revealed the following: The mother, deeply affected by her husband's death, devoted herself completely to the care of the posthumous son, her only child. In her love, she had given in to him ever since he was a baby. It was understandable that he should be indignant when finally a situation arose in which she could not submit to him. And he did what all children do in such cases—he screamed. Since his mother yielded, he became progressively violent and furious whenever anything was denied him. Then his mother realized with horror that he was "just like his father"; and as she had acceded to all her husband's pressing demands, so now she became the slave of her child's whims. With his fits of rage he broke down every resistance. Thus, as a result of her indulgent weakness, she had unknowingly brought up her child to use exactly the same methods which she, in her submissiveness, probably had fostered in her husband.

Attacks of temper may sometimes assume rather terrifying forms, as in the following example:

Four-year-old Frank, an only child, suffered from "respiratory spasms." After initial cries of rage, his breath suddenly gave out; he fell to the floor, became blue in the face, and his body drew up in a spasm. One can imagine the terror of mother and father, who then worked over the boy with damp cloths, picked him up, and carried him around until they were finally able to calm him down with caresses and kisses. These spells were always preceded by an altercation which ensued when the child could not have his way. Afterward, naturally, the parents promised him anything to quiet him.

Despite the menacing aspect of such scenes, tantrums never imply actual danger. They are merely a child's attempt to get his own way; and generally produce prompt results. If the child is left alone, if everyone leaves the room (however loath the anxious and terrified parents may be to do so), the child will recover very speedily of his own accord. If the child is older, he may follow, of course, but as long as nobody pays attention to whatever he may do, his efforts are in vain. An older child may threaten to break windows and furniture, or to throw things at you, a pattern that has been set by previous training. You must keep in mind that broken windows and furniture are not as expensive as a very disturbed child. You must take the chance and leave him alone. If necessary you may have to leave the house. Two or three demonstrations of the inefficacy of his device may be enough to "cure" the child of the dreaded attack. But, of course, we should not forget to mend the deeper injuries caused by previous spoiling, and rectify the derangements of the child's general life plan.

BAD HABITS (THUMB-SUCKING, NOSE-PICKING, NAIL-BITING)

Annoying habits are promoted by the nagging, spite-provoking attitude in parents that we have mentioned so many times before. Many of them are first evoked by this meddling; others, like thumb-sucking, toward which the child is naturally inclined, are only reinforced and prolonged. The same applies to all bad habits—which cannot possibly be enumerated since they are as numerous and varied as are parents' demands. It is always harmful when worried mothers and fathers call special attention to some particular activity. "Sit up straight! Walk straight! Turn your toes out! Don't put your knife in your mouth! Don't put everything in your mouth! Don't make faces!" (One can see that it would be impossible to list all the variants.) These admonitions almost regularly lead to a thorough *cultivation* of the denounced habit—a process indicative of the child's rebellion against parental demands.

Once the habits are established, perhaps without your having anything to do with it, you must consider how to deal with them. We shall take up this matter in connection with the habits that probably are most common and persistent—finger-sucking, nose-picking, nail-biting.

Finger-sucking is by origin not a bad habit, but a natural inclination of the baby. Yet if it continues beyond the first year, you must be careful. It is wrong to pull the child's finger forcibly out of his mouth or to slap him. There are more apt methods that even a baby can understand. You might put gloves on his hands, and, if he has not become especially addicted to sucking as the result of earlier interference on your part, such a move may suffice to spoil his pleasure in the practice. If he commences to put a corner of the bedclothes, or any other available object into his mouth, then you should bear in mind that *the less obvious attention you pay to bad habits, the easier it is to correct them.* If the child is older and you wish to break him of thumb-sucking, you can discuss with him freely his inclination to indulge in easy pleasures. You can emphasize that, after all, this is *his* problem, and not yours; but it may produce deformities in his finger or his teeth and he might not like it later. Such discussions must remain very rare incidents; otherwise you are just nagging. Your main effort should be directed toward helping the child to find better and more wholesome satisfactions. It is either protest against the parents or lack of satisfying activity which keeps the child sucking his thumb. For this reason it is much better to let the child outgrow his finger-sucking instead of interfering in an inadequate way and thereby prolonging the habit.

Nose-picking, too, is among those practices to which all children naturally resort at one time or another. If the child is not refractory to begin with, it often is enough to have a friendly talk with him and point out how ugly and disagreeable the habit is. If you enjoy his confidence, he will believe you and follow your advice. But if you have missed this first opportunity and furthered the habit with exasperated words or actions—in this event you must await a favorable occasion for exerting any educational influence. If you are generally on good terms with the child you may find it possible to enlighten him on the habit in an intimate conversation, when there is complete harmony between you. Often he will agree not to do it any more, but still the practice continues. His defiance vanishes only for this one peaceful hour and may reappear as daily routine. Reproaching him with his inconsistency starts the conflict all over again. It is better to wait until the time arrives for the next friendly discussion. Then he will probably state that he would really like to rid himself of the habit, but simply cannot—he either does it unconsciously, when he is thinking about something else, or finds it impossible to control himself.

In these terms he describes the sham conflict within himself. This can be explained to him calmly and clearly, showing him that he apparently is still not ready to give it up. It is possible through such conversations to approach and solve problems that are of far greater importance to the child's subsequent development and the harmony of the family than the bad habit in and for itself. This technique, naturally, is easier with older, more mature children. In the case of younger children you will probably have to limit yourself to simple, encouraging suggestions. "I am sure you will learn to stop it, just to be polite," or because "it doesn't look nice." "Do you think that maybe you can keep your finger away from your nose all day tomorrow?" If he does not succeed the first day, he may the second or third. These attempts on the child's part should not, of course, be disturbed by inept meddling from other quarters.

As has been said earlier, in breaking children of bad habits you can make good use of *natural consequences*. These can be applied even in the case of a baby. You can tell a child, without offending him, that after he picks his nose you could not possibly let him hold your hands. And you might suggest that probably other people, too, will refuse to give him their hands if they see him pick his nose. Or when he does this, you can get up and leave the room with a remark to the effect that you don't like to watch him. Perhaps your creative imagination will devise still other, similar answers that can be regarded as unpleasant but logical consequences. However, such measures, once adopted, must be maintained and carried out consistently if they are to produce results. Hence it generally suffices to stick to only one of these consequences.

The situation is quite similar with nail-biting. Here again, instruction and natural consequences must supplement each other. This habit betrays obstinacy, rebellion, and tension, and hence occurs usually in combination with other faults. Children who practice it may be sullen, secretive, disorderly, or generally untidy about their persons; in other words, they infringe upon order at a number of points. It seems as though they vent their pent-up anger on their fingers. Sometimes this chronic rebelliousness is compensated, or covered up, in later years by a marked pleasantness; but it still reveals its presence in a variety of faults, or perhaps just in the maintenance of this particular habit. In nail-biting, therefore, particular stress must be laid on general revision of the child's attitude. You should be less concerned with breaking him of the one habit than with extricating him from the conflict-situation. You must try to discover its root—spoiling combined with extreme severity, a feeling of being neglected, or suppressed rivalry with brothers and sisters, and so on. You can accustom the child to order and cleanliness by diverting his ambition toward personal appearance.

However, shaming him about his unsightly fingers is not enough. An inner willingness to look after himself must be awakened. But this result cannot be achieved merely by pressure from without which only increases tension and rebellion. Direct influence, therefore, is of value only when it promotes an inner preparedness for reform. Hence you must pay close attention to the effect of consequences which you introduce, and must take care that they do not increase the child's stubbornness. You must clearly indicate your good will and desire to help. You may suggest, for instance, that he put on gloves when he goes walking with you or when you are to meet friends, because otherwise people might not offer him their hands. You may praise him when you notice that one nail is a little longer than the rest. Sometimes—especially with girls—it does good to have the child's hands manicured. But, first and foremost, every possible source of humiliation, every form of vexation and reproof, must be stringently excluded from the treatment of bad habits.

MASTURBATION

A separate discussion of this "bad habit" is justified only by the exaggerated importance attached to it by overanxious parents, who themselves are usually to blame for its development; for a child who is rightly treated will rarely engage in continual premature sexual activity. Boys who play with their genitals long before puberty generally have been exposed to two kinds of experience: first, to premature sexual stimulation by extreme demonstrations of affection on the mother's part, especially caresses in bed, kissing on the mouth, and close mutual petting (activities which may stimulate sexual sensations

even in three-year-old boys); and second, to parental inter-
vention whenever the child was caught manipulating his genitals. Thus masturbation serves to defy parental power, and
sexual satisfaction becomes a triumph over restrictive order.

It is only natural that every child, in his effort to acquaint
himself with his body, should devote considerable attention to
his sexual organs. This absorption with his body remains un-
injurious as long as it is not noted by the parents. If it is noted
calamity begins. Their own misconceptions and fear of sex-
uality may induce parents to interfere with an activity which
originally was harmless, but which they regard as reprehensi-
ble or even deleterious. Now the well-known cycle begins:
exhortations and slaps lead to increased activity on the child's
part; which increases the determination on the part of the
parents; which again provokes stubborn adherence to the
habit. Now—only *secondarily*, as a result of the conflict—it
becomes a source of surreptitious pleasure. In this way the
genital organs are prematurely stimulated to sensations that
otherwise are reserved for a much later stage in the child's
growth. And then, naturally, the parents' anxiety gets out of
bounds and they resort to terrifying threats, which may seriously injure the child's emotional development.

The struggle against sexual bad habits usually expands later
on into a general conflict. I have seen exasperated, despairing
parents tie the child's hands together above the covers at night
—without success, naturally, for he is cunning enough to cir-
cumvent any violent measure. I have seen attempts to render
his genital parts inaccessible with bandages and appliances,
even with plaster casts! Is it so strange, then, that his interest
in the sexual functions is dangerously enhanced and becomes
the focal point of his thoughts and emotions, sometimes for
the rest of his life?

Such habits can easily be avoided if the parents follow a
strict policy of non-intervention. But once the genital appara-
tus has been prematurely activated, this process can scarcely
be terminated. Yet there is no need for worry. The theory of

damage caused by masturbation has proved to be a false hypothesis. Such practices neither make the child neurotic nor impede his development. There is a relation between masturbation and later nervous complaints, but not as cause and effect. Both are the expressions of a poor attitude toward life and its responsibilities. Masturbation never gives rise to nervousness; but when practiced too early or in excess, it does indicate that the child is uncontrolled, pleasure-seeking, and unable to withstand temptation. These are the faults that require attention, not the incidental sexual play. Overemphasizing the habit provokes the guilt-feeling of the child. The resulting self-accusations and remorse about sexual interests and activities do not stop the child from continuing them, but cause inner tension and conflicts which are much more harmful than the original practices.

UNTRUTHFULNESS

The problem of lying reveals similar mechanisms; an original harmless act can be made into a serious problem through the mismanagement of parents, who permit this fault to become a tool in the contest for respective power.

We must realize that children's "fibs" are not always faults. But they can become so permanent a habit that, for reasons which usually remain a mystery to parents, the deceitful child prefers lying to veracity. All children occasionally deviate from the truth. (Is it different with adults?) There are times when the child's lively imagination makes him unable to distinguish between true and false—that is, reality and fantasy. These phases occur almost regularly between the second and fourth year. Highly imaginative children with vivid daydreams may go through such a stage even later. The child fails to tell the truth either because he believes that his fantasies are real, or he is curious to see what will happen when he puts the fictions of his imagination to the test of reality. Such "lies" may even function as an A.G.M.

This, however, is only *one* source of the child's mendacity. There is no doubt that he also takes an example from the adults of his family and learns to lie when, for instance, he wants to escape punishment or evade a responsibility. Severe parents give abundant provocation for lying. These untruths, then, are simple methods of defense against the exercise of power. Forcible intimidation of children breeds falsehood.

Many parents are terribly upset when they catch their child in a lie. They interpret the child's lie as a serious threat to their power over him. Hence, the more insecure they feel in their authority, the more strongly a falsehood will irritate them. This is not a moral issue, because parents themselves cannot avoid some dishonesty in their own lives. Anxious parents, however, do not admit their concern for their authority, but imagine that the child will degenerate if they permit him to lie with impunity. Accordingly, they bring up the heavy artillery whenever they spot the slightest diversion from the truth. Not infrequently they brand their child as a liar, and thus lead him onto a dangerous road that he would never have followed of his own accord.

You should be careful not to take a lie too tragically. You need not be indignant; your authority is not so feeble that it can be shattered with a single blow. Lying does not make a criminal of the child. Naturally, you should train him to be truthful. But this will never be achieved by scoldings and threats. Vexation and anger only betray your weakness. Many children acquire a liking for falsehoods, since by this means they can baffle the parents. When the child has discovered the power he gains through lying, he lies whenever he feels the need to reduce his parents to helpless despair. His lying no longer springs from specific situations, but is an end in itself. Untruthfulness becomes an expression of the struggle for superiority between child and parent.

The same mechanism can be found in swearing. Children feel big and smart when they use "bad" words, especially when they realize the reaction those words will produce. The surest way to rob a lie of its potential effect is to let it appear as insignificant and trivial, as it really is. Then the child will soon lose his zest for repetitions. He must realize that it gets him nowhere. An understanding smile will make him feel ridiculous and ashamed of himself. But he can be shown that he himself has a vital interest in reciprocal good faith and veracity. *You can never rear your child to truthfulness unless you prove to him that truth is more practical than falsehood.* If he believes the opposite, then neither righteous indignation and sermons nor anger and chastisement are of any avail.

Sometimes a lie of your child may place you in a situation which you do not know how to handle. In all such perplexing situations it is best first to stop and think what you should *not* do (which is much easier to discover!). And simply refrain from any action you should not take; whatever else you do will be adequate. You may also be guided in perplexing situations by the principle of doing the opposite of what the child expects you to do. These considerations will always keep you on the right track. They will prevent you from getting angry, feeling lowered in your prestige, becoming alarmed and frantic. If your children occasionally show off with a lie, you can point out how easy it is to fool you; that if they need such cheap methods to feel important, it is all right with you and you will have to take it. This is a much stronger answer than demonstrating the deep impressions they make on you with a lie.

If they should not respond to such an approach, then you can either devise a game whereby everybody is free to say what he wants, regardless of whether it is true or not. And you, too, can fool them by calling them for dinner when the food is not ready, or pulling other stunts that they won't like. After a while you may propose to them that they might prefer reliability, i.e., trustworthiness. Or you can apply the "wolf! wolf!" story, when the child continues to fib; you just don't believe anything he says after a while. However, if he is un-truthful only to escape punishment or disapproval, you must take it without resentment, for you yourself would very likely lie if you were sufficiently afraid of somebody. And if he lies in order to brag about his importance, you should develop his self-confidence by showing him appreciation and approval so that he will not need to resort to subterfuge to make an im-pression.

DAWDLING

Dawdling is not an offense in itself; but it has a strong effect. It drives some parents to distraction when their child lingers, cannot keep himself busy or amused, and takes an eternity to get one thing done. Dawdling reveals itself as a potent weapon because of the strong reaction that it releases in others. It is an expression of defiance. Here we can clearly see the interplay of child and parent in the development of faulty conduct. For what do parents do when their children dawdle? They remon-strate, urge, become vexed—in short, run the whole gamut of expedients arising from the embittered sense of powerlessness, resulting in an increase of the child's defiance and the conclu-sive adoption of the habit in question. This is the genesis of time-wasting. It grows on the soil of a general passivity and thrives on misguided correctives.

Here again we can see the futility of parental action as long as the child is not understood in his motivation. Few parents stop and think why he behaves in such a way. When the child does not find anything to do and pesters them with questions of what he should do, or when he apparently tries to do some-thing but instead procrastinates, is constantly distracted, or occupies himself with dissipating interests, the parents act on the assumption that he wants to do what he professes or is sup-posed to do. Consequently, they try to remind and press him to finish his job or to do something. But that is not what he de-sires. He may have first looked for their attention; but in the course of the struggle, of their pushing and his resisting, his dawdling becomes directed toward proving his own power, putting the parents into his service, and resisting all their pressure and authority.

What can you do about it? In the first place, the vicious circle has to be broken. No "flying off the handle"! No nagging! However hard it may be, you must learn to observe the child coolly, even when he provokes you. On occasion, you may simply let things pass. If your personal prestige is your main consideration, of course you will retain the old policy; but then you should not be surprised and complain if the child goes from bad to worse. Your first course then, is a negative one: you must avoid false tactics.

There are several positive methods at your command. Since dawdling is a manifestation of defiance and conflict, you would do well to relieve the situation, distract the child's attention, or disconcert him. If you refuse to become irritated and no longer nag him, that above all will set him back on his heels. It is no fun to be slow if nobody gets annoyed! By chatting with him, or arousing his interest in some way, his tendency to dawdle will be lessened. In any case it is essential that you reduce his general hostility by grasping the situation as a whole and helping him out of his difficulties. By such means timewasting can be transformed from a practically hopeless nuisance into a solvable problem.

CHAPTER 3
Taking Revenge

The child who feels unfairly treated and defeated in the struggle for power will want to get even with the parents for what he thinks they have done to him. He has numerous methods which he uses unconsciously to punish and revenge himself upon them. They vary in destructiveness but have in common the amount of anger which they provoke.

STEALING

The horror and despair of parents at the theft committed by their child is easy enough to understand, for stealing reveals how little he regards the clearest and most convincing moral principle. The parents now fear that he will continue inexorably on the road to crime. Most often they try to influence him with severity, with threats and reprisals. They cannot conceive how ineffectual these measures are, or see that in many cases they only hasten and sometimes even give impetus to the dreaded development.

I knew a boy who reacted unusually to the repeated assertion of his mother: "You're bound to be a jailbird and end up on the scaffold." He had a bitter grudge against his parents and was incredibly defiant since he felt, with some reason, that he was slighted in favor of the other children of the family. And so, once when he heard his mother speak these words, he thought, "Not by a long shot! I won't give you that satisfaction!" Gritting his teeth he meticulously did everything that was asked of him, but not without cursing under his breath. He respected all the laws of propriety, but out of his secret antagonism grew an unusually severe compulsion-neurosis.

This reaction to such prophetic utterances is, however, exceptional. There is no surer means of driving a child into the arms of crime than to treat him like a felon and picture him as a future criminal. If we want to help him, we must first know how he came to lose the distinction between mine and thine. This never occurs without deepseated conflicts; but the incidental provocations to steal are various. One child steals because his frivolous nature wants to have immediately whatever his heart desires. He cannot wait. And he does not care about the consequences. When he was small he got everything he wanted, and he cannot see why there should ever be any deviation from this rule. Hence sporadic thievery is common in uncontrolled children who have been too much indulged. It shows an essential want of insight if, at this late hour, the parents stand helpless and terrified before the aberration which their own laxity has induced in their child.

The motives for theft may vary a great deal. Parents rarely detect the real causes. Their perplexity is due to their lack of understanding. The child does not reckon on understanding, since he himself does not understand the reasons for his acts, and so sullenly expects his punishment. When you ask a child why he has stolen you get either stubborn silence or a puzzled "I don't know." It is generally true, the child really does not know why he did it. What he actually knows of his impulses —that he craved candy, fruit, spending money, or other desirable things—is no justification, and he looks for no clemency from admitting it. So he says nothing at all. He himself has not the slightest notion of the deeper motives behind his behavior. But if you want to help the child, you must track these down. You must recognize whether stealing served as an A.G.M., or as a tool for power or revenge.

Horrified and distraught, the mother of eight-year-old Helen appeared at the Guidance Clinic. This carefully nurtured, well-behaved child had, on a number of occasions and with the greatest cleverness, stolen different articles from a stationer's shop—blotting pads, pocket knives, pencils, and the like. She had not been detected until now, so adroitly had she executed the thefts. There seemed to be no reason for her acts. She was given everything she wanted by her mother. When questioned, the girl refused to say why she had stolen or how she had disposed of the articles. Only after we had calmed her fright and tension did we find out that she had distributed the stolen merchandise among her play-mates and school-chums, who had no idea of how they were obtained.

Yet the mystery of little Helen was still far from being solved. Only after we grasped her whole situation, after we learned of the part she played as the youngest child of the family, and realized that she felt insignificant in competition with an older, more capable sister, did the clouds thin; and we saw the light at once. By handing out presents she sought to make an impression on the other children—to cut a figure. And she succeeded nobly. Since she always had some trifle to give away, they all wanted to play or walk with her. How could Helen, who was not aware of these causes and effects, explain why she stole? And can anybody imagine that reproaches and severity could in any way alter her behavior?

Quite different was the case of fifteen-year-old Robert. Here it was much more difficult to understand what moved this fine boy to take valuables and hide them at home. He neither sold them nor boasted of them. His situation, in brief, was the following: His father was very strict, and Robert, the eldest of three children, was particularly closely watched. He had a tendency to take life easy, and allowed himself liberties that his father could not condone. He took walks instead of studying, and failed to come home punctually. He smoked his first cigarette quite early. All in all, he was in obvious revolt against his father. The middle brother, two years younger than Robert, was his opposite. As could be expected, this brother was notably careful and painstaking, and thus became the perfect example of his father's principles.

Robert, too, was unable to say why he stole. His earlier misdemeanors had been rather simple and harmless, but they all evinced his desire to triumph over order and his father. Everything he did was under cover. It was like a secret compensation:

"You see—I do what *I* want, anyway!" Nor was it so senseless that he allowed his stealing to be discovered, for each revelation defied anew his father's ideals. These principles had proved themselves powerless. And herein, apparently, lay the boy's secret aim in life—to demonstrate the futility of the coercion exercised by the social order through his father.

This propensity to snap one's fingers at authority lies at the bottom of a great many criminal acts. It is found even in healthy and respectable individuals. Many "honest citizens" delight in cheating the streetcar company out of the fare. The few pennies probably mean nothing to them, but still they childishly enjoy their "success." To get the better of someone —especially if he is the guardian of order—is not always regarded as dishonorable. This tendency explains many occasional thefts of children. In their eyes there is no essential difference between stealing an apple under the grocer's nose and ringing a doorbell, running off, and gleefully observing from around a corner the wrath of a beslippered paterfamilias. It is true that these are pranks that should not be countenanced, but great moral indignation is wholly out of place. It earmarks the childish stunt as a crime, and may exert a detrimental influence on the child's later development. The most natural consequence is to make the child return the articles.

Naturally, a large theft or the repeated occurrence of less serious acts gives reason enough for earnest consideration of what ought to be done. But so long as you are excited and outraged, you are incapable of helping the child; for then you are not the child's friend and are in no position to understand his situation. Also, it would be a mistake to hold him solely responsible for the trespass. A great part of the responsibility lies with parents, the family constellation, and all the other factors that combine to produce his life situation. In highly problematic cases it may be necessary to enlist the services of a trained outsider—a clinical adviser or a specialist in child guidance. The usual mode of disposing of such incidents—with an excess of anger or despair and feints at punishment—has, among others, the marked disadvantage that it leaves unchanged, or further aggravates, the real situation of the child.

In conclusion, I might point out that children do a great deal of stealing which fortunately never comes to the notice of their families. Although—or because—their parents can take no steps to correct the fault, these children do succeed in becoming respectable people. Is there any one of us who does not have memories of certain childhood transgressions? Even serious offenses need have no unfavorable consequences for the child's development if he is so fortunate as to have friends who use their sympathy and understanding to help him out of his muddled state.

The following example illustrates that stealing may have a great variety of motivations; it also demonstrates how difficult it is to win over a child who has given up hope of being liked and being loved.

Sixteen-year-old Dan was the terror of a social settlement house. Whenever some damage was done at a critical time, he was the instigator. He knew exactly how and when to strike to hurt the most. Once, before a theatrical performance, he ruined all the pianos, actually chopping them to pieces. On another occasion he cut the curtain the night before a performance. He committed endless acts of destruction to property and individuals. His family could not be approached. He was one of a large group of children and was completely ostracized at home. The family got into so many difficulties with and through him—in the neighborhood, in school, at home, with school authorities and police—that they no longer wanted to bother with him.

It was decided to assign him to one of our best and most understanding group workers. The young man made a special effort to win Danny and to get him interested in various activities. He let him help in stage-set construction, gave him responsibilities during the performances, and succeeded in gaining the boy's confidence and cooperation. For quite a while there were no complaints about Dan.

One day the young worker came in great excitement to discuss an episode which puzzled him. He and Dan had been working together when the boy took the worker's watch from the table and put it into his pocket. The worker saw the act but he was not sure whether the boy knew he saw it. At any rate he did not know what to do. He realized it would be a mistake to accuse Danny. So he pretended to look for the watch. Danny volunteered to help him to find it. Finally the worker gave up, saying, "Someone must have taken it." Danny became furious. "Who could do something like that to you! I will look for it; and if I find the guy who took the watch, I will beat him up, but good." So they went around the house asking boys whether they had seen the watch. Danny finally became restless. Suddenly he burst out, "You knew all the time that I had the watch. Why didn't you take it away from me?" And he returned the watch.

The worker had acted correctly. What bothered him was his inability to understand Dan's behavior. Why had he tried this stunt? Apparently Danny could hardly believe that the worker had a real interest in him and was a true friend; he had always been rejected and disliked by everybody. He apparently wanted to see if this particular act would provoke the same treatment which he had experienced all of his life. If the worker had succumbed to the provocation, he would have demanded the return of his watch, perhaps in a sharp way; the boy would have denied taking it, a struggle might have ensued, first with an argument, then perhaps leading to physical violence if the worker had tried to search the boy and to retrieve his watch. Thus the boy would have found his disbelief in friendship justified and reverted to the type of human relationship to which he was accustomed. This act of stealing was apparently a supreme test to which Danny subjected the worker, who passed it with flying colors. One decisive battle was won in the rehabilitation of Danny.

VIOLENCE AND BRUTALITY

The stubborn resistance to order often assumes terrifying forms. Sometimes it is limited to fits of anger, in which case the child retains a certain good will and excuses his eruptions of brutality afterward. But when these outbursts occur frequently and without pretext of being involuntary, the last vestige of good will has vanished and the naked antagonism is revealed. This bold-faced brutality presupposes a mixture of weakness and violent oppression on the side of the mother or father. Intelligent children can develop the most efficient techniques for getting at their parents' vulnerable spots and thus may become a real menace.

Seventeen-year-old Michael lay ill with the flu. His mother did not respond quickly enough to his desires, and he threw three glasses and two plates at her in a single day. When she withdrew, he got up with a temperature of 102 degrees, dressed, and went out on the street. He knew the sure way of reaching his mother's weakness.

Twelve-year-old John was the terror of his family. No one could manage him. He did whatever he pleased: stole money, refused to go to school, lay in bed all one day and stayed out the next day until one in the morning, lashed out at his mother and cursed her like a trooper. But when a stranger was present, someone whom he feared, he was a model of deportment and had a fine talent for explaining everything in a harmless light.

It is obvious that in such cases the blame lies with the parents themselves who, through their indulgence, have allowed the child to get completely out of hand. It is apparent, too, that they did not oppose the rising tide of conflict by pacific and friendly means. Otherwise they would have won him over, and his revolt would never have advanced to this stage. Often enough, the cruelty shown the child is the source of his own brutality. He reflects what he has experienced. Sometimes he may not actually have been abused, but nevertheless felt mistreated. Occasionally, brutality is merely a tool to experience the gratification of complete power over other beings.

Excessive strictness, especially whipping, may stir up rebellion and arouse brutal instincts. These are more likely to arise if one of the parents tries to compensate with compliance for the severity of the other. Neglect may have the same effect. In both cases the child feels more justified in his desire to seek revenge. Before any improvement of the child's behavior can be achieved, the conflict must be ended, at least on the side of the parent. The child must again feel accepted and liked, not feared. If a *natural* consequence cannot be easily and consistently applied, it is as well to do nothing at all. It may make a strong impression on him if he suddenly recognizes that he no longer can intimidate and hurt. Some few experiences of kind firmness may check the child and make him realize the futility of his behavior. They may suffice to reinstate the authority of order. Such effect cannot be attained by blows or other violent measures. If the physical strength or brutality of the child is so great that it is impossible to introduce natural consequences, the child should be removed from his parents and sent to an adequate home, preferably where he would be with several other youngsters. The earlier the parents resign themselves to this fact, the easier it will be for the child to learn to adapt himself to an orderly scheme of existence.

Extreme cruelty and brutality are sometimes observed in young children. The psychological mechanism in these cases seems to be slightly different. Their brutality is directed not so much against parents and against order, as against smaller, "weak" objects, such as animals, younger children, and even inanimate objects. Two factors seem to contribute to such behavior. One is the sensual stimulation produced through acts of violence. Children may have experienced such excitation either personally or by witnessing other children who were beaten, forcibly restricted, or abused. Sometimes stimulation has come from seeing pictures or listening to talk about violent action. Sensual stimulations have a tendency to continue in the same pattern. An experience which once aroused sensual feelings remains associated with the same response. It is sought again as a pleasure device. Sensual desire for brutality may be active or passive (sadistic or masochistic). Children who are frequently exposed to violence are impressed with its excitement. They seek similar sensations by biting or asking to be bitten, by hitting or provoking a blow. They like to suffer or to make others suffer as part of a sensual game. The psychological factors and the proper approach to its readjustment are the same as discussed in the section on sexual play.

Another dynamic factor causing cruelty and brutality in young children is in line with their general style of life. They may try to impress others with their "shocking" behavior (active-destructive A.G.M.), or they may want to demonstrate their power and forcefulness. Brutality against other children is often an expression of "masculinity." "See how strong I am." A desire to punish is frequently just an imitation of parental practices. While playing house, children demonstrate their interpretation of their parents' conduct. Parents who are horrified to see how their child treats his dolls, his "children" or "pupils" in his play, do not realize how the child's behavior reflects their own and how the child's relationship to others is an image of their own relationship to the child.

BED-WETTING

Bed-wetting is seldom due to physical causes, as is often falsely assumed. It is true that organ inferiorities of the bladder, the kidneys, or the spinal cord may facilitate its appearance. There are, however, no diseases which have as their only symptom an inability to retain the urine.

Five-year-old Frank began to wet his bed when his father put him in an orphanage. It never occurred when he slept at home. Eleven-year-old Alan was in conflict with a very strict father. When the latter gave him a severe lecture on school affairs, deprived him of free time, and struck him, the boy started to wet his bed. The purpose of the bed-wetting was very clear in the case of seven-year-old Charles, who went on a long visit to his aunt and, contrary to his previous habits, soiled the bed linen the very first night. When his aunt asked him why he had done this, he said that he only wanted to see whether she would put up with it.

When the antagonism against his environment has reached a certain intensity, the child no longer makes any effort to avoid unpleasantness. His sense of revengefulness is occasionally covered by a masochistic trait of self-abasement. Such children are often ostentatiously dirty. Their whole pride is fixed on *not* washing. They show a "downward ambition" (Wexberg). They achieve a kind of negative glory through the humiliations that they have to suffer, for they are really a sore burden on the entire household. No one knows what to do with them, and the dismay they cause gives them a particular satisfaction. Since this conflict has assumed the form of a physical disorder, it is likely that a doctor has been called in. However, medication will not help. The child must be given back his sense of honor, his faith in himself, and, even more, his faith in people. Heretofore he has been made to feel rejection without knowing that often he himself has provoked it.

But even if it were desirable to treat the symptom for itself, it would be a mistake to awaken the child at night. Apart from the fact that this evidence of concern would increase the satisfaction he receives from his conduct, it must not be the purpose of training to regulate his bladder functions by *outside* help. The child must control his functions of his own accord. Waking the child during the night and putting him on the toilet is not advisable in any event. When the child is awakened during the night, he generally is not fully awake, even if he seems to be. Letting him perform his function in a state of semi-somnolence disturbs rather than stimulates a proper control. Normal control requires full wakefulness; the child must be able to suppress and control his urge until he is fully awakened to take care of himself.

If the training has not been successful in the past, it must now be undertaken in a better way. All you can do is to provide him with a lamp, pajamas, and—if he is old enough—a supply of fresh bed linen so that during the night he can completely take care of himself. He needs encouragement, to be sure. Children who wet the bed are generally deeply discouraged; they are disgusted with themselves and see no hope for improvement. They have to be told that it is up to them whether they want to lie dry or wet, but that they will learn eventually to take care of themselves. Everybody learns it, some sooner, some later. It is of utmost importance that this attitude not only be expressed to the child but actually felt by the parents. As long as the parents themselves are ashamed, disgusted, and desperate, they will of necessity have a bad influence on the child. They will, perhaps, have a false sympathy for him when he is small and relieve him of his natural consequences, for example, by permitting him to sleep in their bed when his is soiled. The first step toward curing bed-wetting is complete calmness and indifference on the side of the parents, who can then successfully attempt to win the child and instill in him new hope and an earnest desire to take care of himself. It is just as harmful to punish him if he is wet, as it is to praise him if he is "nice." That puts too much emphasis on the parents' approval, while it should be strictly his own concern.

CHAPTER 4
Displaying Inadequacy

Children who give up completely in every regard, because they are so discouraged that they do not even move voluntarily, are very rare. In most instances the discouragement is only partial and, as a consequence, the child avoids only certain activities. However, it must be determined whether the child refuses participation in order to gain attention, to defy authority, to punish and hurt, or just because there is nothing to be hoped for. Only in the latter case does a child seek excuses and hides himself behind an inadequacy which may actually exist, but more frequently has been suggested to him by his environment. Sometimes the child assumes an inadequacy out of a wrong interpretation of certain experiences and succeeds in impressing others with it.

INDOLENCE

Indolence is a special form of disorderliness. The child refuses to do his chores, he refuses to cooperate. Everyone has an occasional inclination toward laziness. Children may at times be so immersed in their thoughts, activities, or fantasies that they show no interest in the proceedings of the outside world. Scolding and reproaching a child for his real or supposed indolence will merely increase his unwillingness. One method only is effective—stimulating his interest. Once an interest is aroused, laziness disappears. If a child is so discouraged in schoolwork, for instance, that he considers his efforts futile, he lacks all incentive to action. Children who are left-handed and similarly children who for other reasons are convinced that they are awkward often show an inclination to put off a task. In all these instances it is not enough to arouse interest. The child must be encouraged to develop confidence in his abilities.

Indolence, therefore, is always a sign that the child needs assistance. But this assistance should not be supplied in too literal a sense, as a kind of prop or crutch, in the form of urging and exhorting him to work or, what is worse, performing his tasks for him. This would never aid him in meeting his problems. The help that he really needs consists of discussions and practical experiences which can fortify his self-confidence and strengthen his inner preparedness to apply himself happily and interestedly to tasks and to surmount his difficulties.

STUPIDITY

The child's attempt to evade obligations and to surrender to discouragement may give the impression of stupidity. Many children almost deliberately create this impression. One must consider, of course, the possibility of mental deficiency; but feeble-minded and defective children are rarely called "stupid." The "stupid" child, however, is reproached with his failing, since he is looked upon as normal. His stupidity is not always natural. Often enough it conceals an acquired mental inertness.

Once in a park I witnessed the following scene. A nurse was playing with several girls of about six or seven years of age. One pretty little child came running to her and asked for an apple. She plaintively inquired why the others, who previously had been given two apples apiece, were now presented again with two, while she herself had received only one apple again. The nurse took her on her lap and asked, "How much are one and one?" The happy little face became suddenly distorted and took on a terrified expression; the lips moved without uttering a word.

I knew nothing about this child, but we can sense what lay behind her problem. Could she really count? If not, how did she know the other girls had received two apples at a time? Apparently, it was only the formal "academic" question that she was unable to answer. This would indicate that her stupidity was only a mask. She had probably met with difficulties ever since she started school. Very spoiled children, who have led an easy life at home, often find it hard to adjust themselves to school. They are not used to being on their own. They cannot keep pace with their classmates, and quickly lose courage. Also children who were given a great deal of attention at home because of their charm, their "cuteness," or any other advantage that required no effort, are quite likely to be convinced, when they enter school, that the prescribed work is "too hard" for them. And then they give up; they simply stop trying.

Parents are usually horrified at their child's failure, and thus discourage him still more. Then the process of learning becomes an out-and-out torture to an already unwilling child. He is robbed of his leisure, disturbed at play, and given no peace even at meals. Time after time his parents remind him of his lessons and nag him with queries as to his progress. Is it any wonder that he goes on strike and flatly refuses to apply himself to anything resembling schoolwork? I had a patient once, a woman with an average I.Q., who barely had the formal knowledge of the fourth grade of elementary school. She had been reared in the manner just described, and hence acquired the reputation of being stupid. Yet she was in no way mentally retarded. The only trouble was that she was strikingly beautiful, and had come to depend entirely on her physical attractions. Thus there is such a thing as stupidity induced solely by discouragement. The child fails to learn since he believes himself incapable of understanding anything.

Other children *hide* behind their stupidity. They use "stupidity as an excuse" (Ida Loewy). They "play stupid" when they want to evade some obligation. Children who fail to get along in a particular subject at school will become discouraged; but their discouragement may have various results.

Overambitious children who always want to play first fiddle will not make any effort unless they are sure that they can be on top. When they do not have this certainty they lose interest, claiming that they have no aptitude for the subject, and therefore just cannot learn it.

Even before school age children sometimes play this trick. The little boy who tried to cut his soup with a knife is an example. His parents groaned over his stupidity. Yet he knew well enough what he *should* do—and unfailingly did the opposite. Such children play stupid in order to hoax their parents into waiting on them. Here, too, stupidity is a means of evasion and a device for securing attention.

An only child or a youngest child may employ such tactics when he enters school. In this way he can force his mother to help him with his homework. When she is not sitting by him he can neither write nor do his arithmetic. And the anxious, ambitious mother regularly falls into the trap. She never notices that her child's inability and helplessness increase proportionately as she, surprised and alarmed, makes every effort to encourage him, corrects his mistakes, and ends up by working the problems and writing the themes herself. Some children retain their helplessness throughout their lives and are never capable of writing a letter or paper by themselves. Their minds are a blank when they pick up a pen.

It is not easy to break a child's determination to get the mother's aid and support. When she makes an effort to free herself from her child's domination, he will argue and wheedle. If she remains steadfast and insists that he do his lessons by himself as best he can—then he may come to her with every word or every figure to ask whether it is right. The child may finally agree to work by himself, if his mother will sit by him and watch him.

Accordingly, there are numerous situations in which the child attempts to make use of his stupidity. Analogous to the "play-dead reflex" (often employed by animals to elude their enemies), there is a "play-stupid reflex" that can be observed in children—and sometimes in adults, too. The one "reflex" generally serves its purpose of evasion as well as the other. For, in effect, the family and the environment generally do nothing to combat the real or apparent stupidity, but rather acknowledge its efficacy as means of evasion. Parents scold, criticize, and humiliate the child but at the same time they unwittingly fall for his trick; for, in the end, they relieve him of the work that he wants to avoid, or they put themselves into his service. They encourage his stupidity by their criticism and ridicule, which strengthen one of the main factors that produce stupidity, that is the child's dependence, his lack of faith in his own ability.

How then, should one deal with a "stupid" child? It certainly requires a change in the attitude of the parents. They will have to stop scolding, confronting him with his incapacity, teasing and comparing him with a brilliant brother or sister; but they will also have to stop their laxity in allowing him to shirk his duties. That cannot be accomplished by urging and threatening, which makes a distasteful task even more disagreeable to the child. He should be made to feel the consequences of his dereliction. As matters stand, the *parents* feel punished when he fails, not he. Therefore, they try to prevent the unpleasant consequences. As a result, the child feels that he has to meet his obligations for the parents' sake, not for his own. Their concern over his progress relieves him of his own responsibility. If he fails in school, he punishes the parents.

It is the duty of the teacher to stimulate his interests, and parents should interfere as little as possible with schoolwork. However, they can help a great deal by stimulating the general interest and alertness of the child through interesting books, excursions to museums and zoos, through nature stories, and other discussions suitable to his age and development. Then he may take a greater interest in the corresponding school subject and find pleasure in his work.

Eight-year-old Rose is too "stupid" to play with other children. She cannot dress or undress herself or even speak properly. She swallows half her words and syllables. It goes without saying that she is behind in school. She is considered retarded and is so treated, although she is not feeble-minded and has an I.Q. of 91. When it comes to getting her own way, she is shrewd and even ingenious in maintaining an advantage once gained. She is never at a loss for an answer. Rose has a very clever sister who is one and one half years younger than she. The sister outshines her in every way; but Rose compensates through all the attention she gets. She even has her own nurse and, when she started school, got a private teacher. Stupidity often pays big dividends! Less fortunate children are just thrown overboard and left completely to themselves.

There are a great number of children with a low I.Q. who are for all practical purposes retarded and still are only pseudo-feeble-minded. They have either a brother or sister, usually the next older or younger one, who is extremely bright and excels intellectually and academically. His or her superior abilities discourage the other to such a degree that he gives up completely. Sometimes this total surrender is due to an extremely efficient mother or older sister, who takes full charge of everything so that there is nothing left for the child to do.

Proper treatment can do a great deal for children whose intelligence is under question. They sometimes blossom overnight and reach achievements which nobody had believed were possible for them. Even the I.Q. increases, to the discomfort of those who consider it unchangeable. Unfortunately, the differential diagnosis between true feeble-mindedness and pseudo-retardation can often be made only afterward, by the success or failure of the treatment. For this reason, a low I.Q. should never deter parents and teachers from taking every step possible to help the child. On the contrary, it should be an incentive to employ better and more effective methods to make use of the remaining aptitudes so that the child can become a useful member of the human society.

"INAPTITUDE"

A "natural" inaptitude is often assumed if a child notably lacks some ability. This assumption becomes a conviction if every effort to improve the child's deficiencies fails, especially if he himself seems to try hard.

The acquisition of skills and abilities is a complicated process. It requires considerable practice and training. Unfortunately, scientific insight into all the factors which affect the course of training, favorably or adversely, is in the earliest stages of development. Many inaptitudes and deficiencies are the result of unrecognized errors and oversights in the training of the child.

How can we stimulate a child to develop his latent potentialities? It is impossible to list all the methods. The issue becomes further confused because the same stimulation may produce the opposite effect in different children. The example of father and mother may stimulate one child to emulate them, and discourage another one who feels incapable of ever reaching their level. High expectations stimulate one child and hamper another one. Objections and prohibitions act like natural obstacles and organ inferiorities, impelling one child to special efforts and preventing another one from doing anything. Opposition or conformity, defiance or submission, self-confidence or discouragement, determine whether any given stimulation has a constructive or detrimental effect.

This bewildering diversity is responsible for the lack of clarity in the methods of fostering abilities and for the inclination to assume hereditary predisposition for certain skills. For this reason, many parents and teachers, as well as some psychologists, regard inaptitudes and deficiencies as the result of a lack of endowment. Examination of children and adults reveals, however, that improper training coupled with discouragement must be considered the main factor. One can always find the point in the training at which the child gave up. Some children never learn spelling. They are those who got so discouraged when they started school that they abandoned all effort. Others give up because they cannot excel. Certain children who are used to having their own way are not willing to agree that a word *must* always be spelled in the same way. They spell it as they are inclined to, once in one way, the next moment in another way. They finally get so confused that they no longer attempt to find out how the word should be spelled. There are many well-educated and well-read adults who have never learned to spell because their first teacher was unable to overcome their growing inferiority in regard to spelling; and now as grown-ups they are still frightened if they have to write a letter.

The inability to master mathematics may be due to an incidental initial discouragement in the process of studying. Some overprotected children never learn to make their own decisions; they find it difficult to solve any mathematical problem which demands decisions in regard to procedure. These children may be excellent students in subjects where they can rely on information. But any activity that requires self-reliance and determination is closed to them.

I should like to demonstrate this fact in a field that heretofore has been looked upon as the exclusive domain of natural endowment—musical talent. There are people who take no pleasure at all in music, for whom it is even a torment. They may be "monotones," unable to sing even simple tunes —this generally is taken to indicate a complete lack of musical ability. But it has been proved in a great many instances that the assumed "lack of a musical ear" is nothing but a protest against musical activity as a result of discouragement— sometimes because of competition with an older sister or some other member of the family who showed a pronounced musical talent. Frequently, the typical contrast between first and second child leads to such "deficiencies."

When Eric was ten years old he seemed to be wholly unmusical. He could not be induced to listen to concerts and was incapable of singing even the simplest nursery songs. In his infancy he had shown some interest in music, but later he completely reversed his attitude. His father often conducted musicales in the home. The boy, who as an only child, had been spoiled by his mother, would not sit still while the music was being played, and finally had to be sent out of the room. From this time on he could not bear music. When he entered school he refused to sing with the others and was reprimanded and ridiculed. When his grandmother tried to teach him songs, he became irate and ran away. After he was ten the reasons for his attitude were carefully explained to him, and through his new understanding he was helped to overcome his antagonism to music. With the aid of an understanding teacher, he developed a "fine ear" and learned to sing very well.

Children who have never been taught to sing at home may be stigmatized as unmusical when they attempt to join in the unison singing at school and fail. They are impressed and dejected by the superior ability of their classmates, and their discouragement may easily be increased by thoughtless teachers who ridicule them, until in the end their want of musical ability is taken as an established fact, persisting despite all pseudo-effort and pseudo-practice. In later years—but perhaps not until quite late in life—such persons may finally be brought to realize that their lack of musical ability was a fiction, that they, like anyone else, can acquire a taste and a feeling for music. And then their "natural" inaptitude will come to a sudden and miraculous end.

The natural inclination of children toward music is often stifled by the parents' attitude in regard to practicing. Ambitious parents may insist that their children practice more. Little do they realize the damage which they do thereby to the musical development of their children. They transform an art which should provide enjoyment and inspiration into a tortuous and tedious task. To be sure, nothing can be achieved without training; but training requires *interest* and *stimulation*. Going through the motions of practicing will not do. The usual method of coaxing, reminding, threatening, and punishing certainly does not provide either stimulation of interest nor inspiration. It is up to the teacher to interest the child; parents should add stimulation, but not pressure. They can play records or take the child to concerts; they can help the child to appreciate good music; they can admire his progress. Of course, they can force him to sit at the piano, but in most cases they thereby kill his musical enthusiasm. When he fails as a result, they—and sometimes even the teacher—blame it on the lack of musical ability. Actually the conflict between parents and child and the ensuing wrong working habits of the child prevent proper training. His inability is the result.

A rather detailed discussion of musical talent has seemed appropriate since it shows so clearly how loosely and thoughtlessly the concepts of heredity and predisposition are accepted. Such pessimistic assumptions induce parents to increase the difficulties for the child instead of helping him to overcome them. Musical talent is quite analogous to all the specialized endowments. If a child seems to lack ability in drawing or composition, mathematics, languages, or other school subjects, one should first try to determine whether he has been discouraged and, if so, how; or whether and why he resists the demands of training. Persuasion and urging will of course have no more effect on him than scolding, fault-finding or, what is worse, exaggerating his supposed inaptitudes—all of which would only drive him further along the road toward failure. Raising the child's confidence, winning him over and thus overcoming his resistance, letting him realize his progress, strengthening his self-reliance, stimulating his interest and enthusiasm, and, above all, exercising patience throughout the necessary process of training—these are the means that often can rectify deficiencies that once seemed hopeless.

On the other hand, it is not feasible deliberately to create special abilities in the child. A particular talent develops only in the soil of a highly concentrated and intensive training, and this can hardly be imposed from without. Ambition will sometimes spur a child to exceptional attainments; but quite often it may lead him to shun activity if his courage and self-confidence do not balance his aspirations. In any event, one should keep a close check on his attitude toward his work, and advance his progress by means of encouragement. Many overzealous parents induce their child at an early age to a strenuous activity that gives promise of really remarkable achievements. For a time he may seem a prodigy, the fulfillment of all their expectations; but in far too many cases the ultimate result is collapse and wretchedness. Later generations of parents will perhaps renounce the methods that arouse antagonism and lead to discouragement, and they may have better success in drawing out the dormant potentialities of their children.

"VIOLENT" PASSIVITY

Children who are completely passive are very rare. Even children who are very dull and develop no abilities, either physical or mental, may show some active participation. The strongest impression of passivity is given by children who use their passivity deliberately as a means of resistance. True enough, they are discouraged and have given up in despair; however, their passivity is so strong that one can speak of it as "violent" passivity. These children show some signs of a desire for power and especially of vengeance; but their goals are achieved solely by passive methods. They drive parents— and teachers even more—to utter despair. There seems just nothing one can do to move them. One literally hits rock if one tries to influence or direct them.

John, nine years old, was brought to the Center because he refused to cooperate either at home or in school. He did not actually get into mischief, although he occasionally transgressed by lying, stealing, truancy, and the like. He offended more through what he did not do. He was lazy, very untidy and dirty, went to school half dressed, and was usually tardy. He failed in almost all subjects, did not do any homework; nor did he make any effort to pass his tests. He did not even play, either with his siblings or with other children. He was shoved around at home, constantly coaxed, threatened, and severely punished—without any effect. His behavior had become worse in the last two years. The decisive factor in his development was his brother, one year younger, who had surpassed him at home as well as in school. His brother was by no means a good student, but he passed; and John's behavior grew worse when his brother entered into the same grade and later stepped one grade ahead of him.

The first day at the Center John refused to come to the counseling room. The next time he came in with his mother but remained at the door. No invitation, kindly suggestion, or coaxing made any impression upon him. We let him stay there, and could observe that during the session his face revealed an interest in the proceedings. At the next session he was willing to sit down near the doctor, but he did not say one word, although he understood and responded with occasional smiles and slight gestures. When it was time for him to leave the room so that we could talk with his mother, he refused. He just did not get up. He had to be carried out on the chair, and he accepted this without any resistance.

John's violent passivity was eventually overcome by methods similar to those employed with children who show their power. The mother, a tense, rigid, and highly perfectionistic person who had punished him a great deal and even spanked him severely when he was slow and late to school, learned to restrain herself and instead to apply the natural consequences. John's first active participation was in a rhythm band at the Center. It was his first experience of pleasant cooperation with others. Later he joined a dancing class. In the meantime, he became more and more cooperative and friendly at the Guidance Center, expressing himself with increasing frankness and ease, and finally began to apply himself in the classroom. It was only natural that at this point his brother began to get into difficulties.

Forcefulness in fighting with passivity is even more impressive if it is limited.

Seven-year-old Jack refuses to talk except with his mother, who pampers him a great deal and submits to his whims. But that is the only relationship which Jack apparently accepts. At school he just does not say a word. He has learned to write and is willing to answer the teacher's questions in writing; he may make himself understood by gestures and signs, but he will not utter a word. He is outwardly conforming when addressed—he will do what he is told, but will not answer a question. At the Center he stares into space as if he could not hear what is said. He completely ignores communication.

As was stated before, it is questionable whether children who resort to violent passivity really belong in the fourth group. Their passivity seems sometimes to be more than just giving up. One should recognize the power element in doing nothing. Any pressure, coaxing, or punishment makes the child only more determined in his non-participation. The best response to his behavior is to leave him alone in such a way that he experiences the unpleasant effect of his passivity. As long as he can force the parents' hand and stimulate them to more activity and effort the child will find his method only too successful and comfortable.

CHAPTER 5
Pathological Reactions

The resistance of the child may develop to such a degree that he may seem to be "abnormal." However, one must be careful what one considers pathological or abnormal in a child. As a rule, the child's reactions are not abnormal, even if they are extreme and seem out of the ordinary, because they are generally sensible and adequate responses to the situation as the child sees it. However, what is "normal" for the child may become "pathological" when it is carried into adult life where the reaction is no longer in accordance with the actual situation. Even if a child is quite different from the ordinary, he should not be called pathological, because such designation generally is based on a lack of insight into his relationships to parents, teachers, or society as a whole.

The term "pathological reaction" is justified only in describing certain reaction patterns, which, if they should be maintained in later life, would become typical psychopathological conditions. We can observe in children the first characteristic signs of these conditions, and case histories of adult patients reveal that often the first symptoms had appeared in early childhood. Such symptoms in children do not justify apprehension, fear, and pessimism. However, while some symptoms justify special care and consideration to prevent a continuation leading to pathological conditions, the parents, motivated by these emotions, may become more detrimental to an already disturbed adjustment.

NERVOUS DISORDERS

We have already cited typical neurotic mechanisms frequently found in children when we discussed fear, overconscientiousness, temper tantrums, and the lack of concentration. Characteristic of every neurotic disturbance, in children and adults alike, is the tendency to maintain good intentions and to hide antagonism behind "symptoms" that are used as alibis. The child may have used these symptoms originally to excuse himself to the parents; but as soon as he believes his own excuses, the neurotic mechanism is established.

Many nervous symptoms may appear in early childhood. They are always aimed against the parent and against order. The child tries in this way to throw off certain responsibilities and secure consideration and assistance, or sometimes merely increased attention. The symptoms, accordingly, vary with the circumstances. They often follow the example that the child sees, and may be stimulated by casual experiences. *The development of a symptom depends on the manner in which the family reacts to its first appearance.* The stronger the effect that a symptom produces, the greater the likelihood of its further development. Ignoring it hastens its disappearance—at least in the beginning, when it is not yet firmly established.

Characteristic of the nervous child is the *tension* under which he lives. This arises from the difficulties with which he has to contend: from conflicts with parents, siblings, and teachers, from the dangers that threaten, from inordinate ambition. His whole organism is under the pressure of this strain; and thus any thought and emotion, any function of bodily organs to which his attention is directed, can develop into a nervous symptom. After whooping cough, the irritation may persist much longer than is warranted by the normal course of the illness; a stomach disorder caused by unwholesome foods may be maintained or repeated; cardiac complaint in the mother may lead the child to watch his own pulse and acquire nervous heart trouble. It is especially noteworthy that the nervous disorders of others are readily imitated by the child. And here again the family's perturbation over a disturbance—which is often regarded at first as a mere "bad habit"—encourages the child to adopt it permanently.

It is impossible to give even an approximate list of the neurotic disorders that appear in children. We shall briefly indicate a few.

A direct expression of tension is the so-called spasm. Spasms may appear in any muscular group, either over the entire body (in which case they are often falsely described as epileptic or heart attacks) or restricted to the eyelids (blepharospasm), the musculature of the jaw (trism), the facial muscles (*tic convulsif*, which leads to grimaces), the muscles of the throat and neck, or the shoulder, arm, and leg musculature. They may appear as yawning, sneezing, laughing, and crying fits or as coughing spasms. Since sometimes these accompany a real physical complaint, a general medical examination is advisable in every case.

Tension can easily lead to nervous derangements of the gastrointestinal tract. Nervous children cannot eat when they are overwrought—before a trip, before going to the theater, and when anything disagreeable is in the offing. Going to school also affords opportunity, and for this reason breakfast may be difficult. Perhaps the child is in opposition to school, or he is very ambitious and dreads failure. In either event he seems incapable of taking nourishment in the mornings, especially before an examination or an unusual assignment. Coaxing may cause stomach spasms or nervous vomiting. The cramping of the pyloric orifice (pylorospasm) is often connected with reluctance to take food. Tension of the gastrointestinal tract may lead to diarrhea or constipation.

Extreme tension may disturb the child's sleep. He tosses

restlessly and screams or sometimes talks in his sleep. His brain still works on the problems that fill his daily life and give rise to emotional upheaval. Or perhaps he cannot sleep at all, because he is too much occupied with his problems. The vascular system reacts readily to strain, since anxiety and cardiac activity are interrelated in a physiological fear-mechanism. The results are palpitation, accelerated pulse-beat, blushing, and pallor—also increased sweat secretion, together with fear-sensations. Children exposed to much moral pressure may develop compulsive-obsessive symptoms.

The therapy consists first of quieting the child and above all, the parents. In cases of extreme excitement, medication does some good, but only as a temporary relief of the specific symptom. What was said earlier of children's faults is equally true of their nervous disorders: It is futile to treat only the symptom. *The child's personality and his relationship to the parents must be altered.* His whole situation needs drastic revision. Even ignoring the symptom checks the development of only one particular manifestation. The general strain is not affected. In difficult cases, especially with older children, psychotherapeutic treatment is indispensable. But it is not enough to help the child out of his present predicament; treatment must include the parents and induce them to adopt a more sensible attitude.

PSYCHOSIS

The number of children who are classified today as psychotic is increasing. This may be due to the fact that heretofore they were not recognized as being different from severely retarded children. Actually, there are indications that these children, acting very much as if they were mentally deficient, have normal and often superior intelligence. Since their behavior seems to be utterly irrational and cannot be controlled with reason, they are called psychotic, often schizophrenic. However, their mental condition is quite different from that of adult schizophrenics, although they too seem to live in a world of their own, apparently little affected by events in their environment. Their distance and lack of contact are often expressed not only by their unwillingness to listen but also by their inability to talk. Many of them are completely mute, and many seem to be deaf, while actually having no hearing defect. Because the nature of their "psychosis" is so little understood and because of the stigma attached to this term, these children are often not called psychotic, but "emotionally retarded."

No generally accepted explanation of the origin of this condition has been established. Some experts attribute it to an organic brain deficiency, particularly to a defective development; others consider the personality of the parents, particularly of the mother, as the cause of this form of abnormality. Our own observation would indicate that the parents of so-called psychotic children are not much different from those of normal children and—as a matter of fact—very often have other, completely normal children. On the other hand, the assumption of an organic deficiency becomes dubious when we see—so far in only a few cases—a complete recovery and adjustment. It may be possible that these children have what may be called an organ inferiority of the brain which makes them more susceptible to certain patterns of behavior.

The outstanding feature of all these children is the determination to have their own way and to disregard any pressure and demand from the outside. This resistance to pressure prompted some experts to assume that treatment should avoid any pressure. Our observations lead to opposite conclusions. Permissiveness usually intensifies the condition, while persistent firmness reduces the violence often exhibited. It is this determination of the child to resist the power of an authority, be it exerted by an individual or by the demands of the social situation, that may provide the clue to an understanding of this condition.

It seems to be a counterpart of the other extreme form of youthful rebellion, namely juvenile delinquency. Both occur to an extended degree at a time when parental authority diminishes in a democratic setting and heretofore submissive children dare to express their defiance openly. In other words, childhood psychosis seems to indicate the extreme rebellion of a child who no longer fears retaliation and punishment or at least takes it in his stride as the price for his perverted form of independence. This open rebellion is only possible in an era of parental overpermissiveness, when parents are no longer able and willing to "control" children. But it probably requires some organic predisposition for a child to let his inclinations sway him without any inner control.

There is little to be said about the prevention of such a mental state, except for pointing to the need for order and regularity within the family. This no longer can be brought about by direct pressure but requires the wide range of training methods described in this book. The vulnerable, sick, or physically defective or handicapped child does not need any special methods of training, only a more careful observance of the basic principles. On the other hand, all handicaps and deficiencies make the maintenance of proper attitudes and procedures more difficult and therefore demand from the parents more determination and perseverance in using the proper approaches.

Once a psychotic condition has developed, psychiatric help is needed. New drugs have been developed that influence the child in such a way as to make training methods more effective. These drugs do not cure the child but make him manageable; and the proper retraining then, in turn, may take its effect and permit either complete or partial adjustment. It is our experience that music therapy can often reach a child when all other therapeutic efforts have failed. Psychotic children are usually immune to a verbal approach, but the nonverbal approach of music can induce participation and contact. The rhythm also contributes to the therapeutic effectiveness of music. It implies order in a form to which the child can easily and more readily respond.

As in all severe power contests, the parents of a psychotic child need to be able to extricate themselves from the child's undue demands. It requires considerable fortitude to resist firmly but calmly the often considerable, vicious aggressiveness of such children. For the sake of maintaining their own independence and self-dignity, parents must have the fortitude and courage to stand up for their own rights and not to submit to the force of a sick child. Justifying a false considerateness and permissiveness on the grounds that "the poor child is sick" induces a child to become even more sick and to use his sickness as a club over his victims.

PSYCHOPATHIC PERSONALITY

A misbehaving and rebellious young child may behave like a psychopathic personality without actually being one.[1] He does not share the values and moral concepts of the rest of the group to which he belongs. He may be defiant or self-indulgent; he may demand his own way and be completely unwilling to conform. However, a great number of these children, one may say the vast majority of them, adjust them-

[1] A psychopathic personality, as we understand it, can be defined as a person who has not developed an adequate conscience and does not accept the morals and values of the society in which he lives. Consequently, his behavior is socially disturbing. He considers his own interests as the only motivation which matters, without inhibition and restraint. We can distinguish three groups of psychopathic personalities: (1) the Indulgent Personalities—the alcohol and drug addicts, the gamblers, the liars, the perverts, the swindlers, the eccentric, the malingerers; then there are (2) the Defiant Personalities—the criminals and delinquents, the morally insane, the active sex offenders and prostitutes, the impulsive and quarrelsome; in this group belong (3) some Mentally Deficient Personalities, who have not learned to recognize right and wrong and have a limited knowledge of good and bad. They may be indulgent, defiant, or merely nonconforming, uninhibited, and impulsive.

selves later on without displaying any psychopathic tendencies. While their adjustment to home and school may have been inadequate, they succeed in adjusting themselves to society at large during the period of adolescence, once they become independent of those family relationships which disturbed their adjustment. On the other hand, children who did not previously show any obvious sign of nonconformity may be inclined to defiance during puberty if home and school either interfere with or neglect the necessary assistance and supervision. The resulting juvenile delinquency is largely a product of the lack of preparation for adolescence and of the inability of educational institutions like home and school to understand, appreciate, and stimulate the adolescent youngsters in proper channels.

Any trend to nonconformity and non-participation must be recognized and watched in children. It cannot be suppressed by force, or mitigated by indulgence. These two methods of indulgence and suppression, applied predominantly today to misbehaving children, are mainly responsible for the great number of self-indulgent and defiant personalities. As long as schools cannot make up for this deficiency by winning the children over, integrating them in a harmonious way into the group, and adjusting them to order, psychopathic personalities will develop in ever-increasing number, especially in periods of change. The changing values of our time favor the defiance of moral concepts presented by parents and authorities. The more justified the children feel in rejecting the values of their parents, the more defiant they may grow in rejecting any moral value. Again it must be stated that such turmoil during puberty, which may even lead to delinquency, does not necessarily mean continuation of these psychopathic traits. However, punitive action by the authorities and overindulgence or neglect by the parents may drive the youngster deeper into social antagonism until finally his return to social participation may be permanently blocked.

Some children develop serious psychopathic traits of extreme defiance or extreme indulgence during puberty, some much earlier. The sex impulse may stimulate defiance and indulgence simultaneously. Such children may get completely out of control, as no force of parents or authorities is strong enough to prevent the victories of defiance. Gambling and drinking, vandalism, and uncontrollable self-indulgence in any kind of fun and pleasure, culminating in arson and rape, mark the development of a child who seeks significance outside the social order and the adult society.

It is unfair to blame parents alone for the increase in juvenile delinquency. After all, who helps the parents today in their superhuman task of raising children? Teachers, juvenile authorities, police, and courts equally must learn to understand the individual delinquent and his problems. A better understanding of those who have already come into conflict with the law may aid greatly in the public planning for the prevention of juvenile delinquency. Most of the youngsters with psychopathic traits are very ambitious but do not find adequate outlets in useful accomplishments. They want to be big and smart, and gain this objective more easily through misbehavior than through conformity. It is easier for them to feel grown up and important by emulating the vices of the adults than by fulfilling their tasks which, generally, offer them little recognition in the world of adults.

Once a child has turned against adults, it is difficult to influence him in a direct way. He is generally backed up by his contemporaries who think and feel as he does, since he can pick just those mates whose attitudes jibe with his. Therefore, remedial work with individual parents and children is not too efficacious; group approaches through new activities and especially through group discussions are much more promising. In that way it may be possible to influence and improve the social values and concepts of the whole group. It is easier to influence the group than it is to influence one individual, as one can find assistance from members within the group which can serve as a foundation on which to build.

As the psychopathic personality is characterized by denial of the social values of others and by exclusive consideration of one's own interest, the problem of mental retardation becomes necessarily related to it. It is true that some children are prevented by actual lack of intellectual capacity from grasping fully the more complex concepts of morals and values. But while children with extensive mental deficiencies are generally prevented from mixing with others and from doing damage to others and to themselves, children with a lesser deficiency can be a real danger. Many mentally deficient children, if carefully trained, stimulated, and supervised, could very well learn to participate adequately and even successfully in life. However, under present educational conditions, unsatisfactory at best, the additional problem of mental deficiency is too much for parents and teachers. Instead of getting better care, these children get far less training and sometimes none at all. Long before they enter school their limited abilities are already stifled through spoiling, overprotection, or neglect. It is true that training such children is difficult and does not promise any return comparable to the training of average or above average children. However, society as a whole pays a high price for its neglect in handling and training retarded children, through the part which they play in delinquency.

Concluding the discussion of the most disturbed children, we must call attention to the prevailing conditions under which they grow up. One can say: the more help and assistance a child needs, the less he receives. Proper treatment and stimulation on the part of parents, teachers, and others is given only to those who need the least, because they are well adjusted and can take care of themselves. They are treated with all the affection, attention, and consideration to which every child has a right. On the other hand, the most disturbed child receives the worst treatment, little or no understanding, assistance, and encouragement. He is pushed around, abused, humiliated, and driven into deeper rebellion and discouragement. This prevalent paradox can be overcome only through a wider knowledge of efficient training techniques and through a better preparation for the understanding of the personality of each child.

PART II
CASE ILLUSTRATIONS

It is hoped that the foregoing presentation has helped you to recognize several of your mistakes, to gain a better understanding of your child, and perhaps even to improve your relationship with him. But you may still feel a need for further direction, especially if your own emotional equilibrium has been too upset or the child's behavior too disturbing. You may want to know about specific techniques used in guiding parents and children to a mutually constructive relationship. A discussion of actual cases treated in a guidance center will demonstrate how remedial techniques are used and may give you a clearer understanding of the methods I have attempted to describe in this book. Some of these techniques may be applicable to your own situation or may stimulate you to further thought and solutions. Perhaps you may decide to consult a similar center in your own community if you feel a need for professional assistance of the kind described.

Most parents know so little about the management of their children that outside help is essential in a great many instances. Teachers, too, are as a rule little prepared to understand fully a child who disturbs and misbehaves. Consequently, a great number of children need help beyond that which the classroom can provide. The fact that a child requires special assistance does not in any way indicate the presence of a pathological condition. A child becomes a problem only if parents and teachers do not know how to handle the problems which he presents. Not only does the child need assistance, but parents, too, require the objectivity of professional counsel. Their inefficiency in dealing with the child's problems is not their fault and does not necessarily indicate their inadequacy. But so long as parents and teachers lack proper preparation and training we must recognize the necessity for establishing agencies which are qualified to give the required assistance. Such agencies, serving the needs of parents, children, and teachers are commonly called Child Guidance Clinics. Their staff usually consists of a psychiatrist, a psychologist, and a social worker.

The appellation "Child Guidance Clinic" should, perhaps, be reconsidered. The word clinic generally implies a medical institution for the treatment of disease. As the function of Child Guidance Clinics is increasingly directed toward helping the *normal* child in his adjustment and growth, the term "Guidance Center" is more appropriate. (In Austria such institutions were called *Erziehungsberatungsstellen,* which means, literally translated, "centers for advice in rearing children.") In the future, we may very well have to distinguish between two types of Guidance Center: one, a clinic which deals mainly with extreme cases, where the disturbance is so severe that it may be called pathological and requires special treatment and management; and a Guidance Center for parents and children which serves the needs of the average parent, child, and teacher. Such Centers should be established in each community under public or private sponsorship, within the school system, and/or in community and settlement houses, churches, and similar institutions.

Various techniques of clinical guidance are used at the present time. Alfred Adler and his associates developed a particular technique for use in Guidance Centers. Its main principles are:

1. The focus of attention is directed toward the parent, as the parent is generally the problem, not the child. The child responds only to the treatment to which he is exposed. Younger

children, especially, cannot be helped as long as the parents' attitude does not change.

2. All parents consulting the Center participate simultaneously in a procedure that may be called "group therapy." In these sessions each case is openly discussed in front of the other parents. Any initial objection to such group participation disappears quickly when, at the first interview, the parents realize the spirit of mutual help and understanding. Confidential or embarrassing material is never brought up in the group, but is discussed at private interviews with the social worker or the psychiatrist, as the case requires. The advantage of group discussions is soon evident to any newcomer. Most parents gain greater insight into their own situation by listening to the discussion of problems of other parents, for it is easier to be objective in evaluating and understanding other people's problems.

3. The same guidance worker, whether psychiatrist, social worker, or psychologist, deals with the parents and with the child. All problems of children are problems of a disturbed parent-child relationship. In any case, the worker is confronted with a particular relationship and must approach it from both ends simultaneously. We have never felt any particular resistance by parent or child because we dealt with both; it is as easy to gain the confidence of both parties as that of the one. Our experience has indicated that working with one party alone is almost a handicap. The speed and course of the treatment depend upon the condition and receptivity of parent and child at a given moment; and these can be evaluated only if the worker is in close contact with both.

4. The problems of the child are frankly discussed with the child himself, regardless of his age. If the child understands the words, he also understands their psychological content. Contrary to a widespread belief, young children show amazing keenness in grasping and accepting psychological explanations. In general, it takes much longer for a parent to understand the psychological mechanisms of the problem; the child recognizes

them immediately. It is not that the child is more suggestible and therefore more easily "taken in" by suggestive remarks; his "recognition reflex" appears only when an interpretation is correct.

The child is called to the counseling room without his parent, and by his actions, his behavior, and his responses reveals his attitudes and characteristic approaches to life. The discussion is brief and directly attacks the basic problems; if it strikes home it generally makes a deep and lasting impression. Children are rarely embarrassed by the presence of adults; but, even if they are, they reveal in these difficult test situations more of their basic attitudes and reaction patterns, more of the true nature of their problems, than they do in "normal" situations at home or in their classrooms, where their true motivations may be covered up by compensatory and deeply entrenched behavior patterns.[1] Psychological tests are given if the diagnosis is not clear or special information seems necessary, but only few cases require such tests.

5. If the child is not an only child, we never deal with him alone. Each child in the family plays an important part, as the problem of any one child in the family is closely related to that of every other member of the group. We have to understand the whole group and the existing interrelationships, the lines of alliance, competition, and antagonism, really to understand the concepts and behavior of any one member. For this reason, we ask the parents to bring all their children.

When the children enter the guidance room, they are asked to sit together on a bench. The way in which they enter the room, how they sit down, their distribution and position on the bench, the way in which each one participates in the discussion, their facial expressions and other reactions during the discussion—all are definite clues to the relationships existing among them. This effort to deal with all of them simultaneously is the more necessary as any change which may be accomplished in one child is bound to affect the whole group sit-

[1] See below, case history of "The 'Teeter-Totter' Brothers."

uation. Often enough, if the "problem child" improves, the "good one" who is his more successful competitor becomes difficult. In many cases one can clearly see that the child with whom the parents have the greatest difficulty is not really the maladjusted one. At any rate, we cannot help any one child unless we establish a better equilibrium among all the children. The change in their relationships must be closely watched and the necessary steps taken to improve the attitudes of each child toward the group.

6. The main objective of our work is the change in the relationships between child and parent, and between the siblings. Only then can we alter the child's behavior, his life style, his approaches to social living, his concepts of himself in relation to others. The psychological guidance in each case is based on the interpretation of his family constellation and on the recognition of his goals. His difficulties are caused by his trying to gain attention (goal 1), to demonstrate his power (goal 2), to punish or get even (goal 3), or to demonstrate his inadequacy (goal 4).

The first interview at the Center (after the social worker presents the case history) is generally devoted to an explanation of the psychological factors behind the problem. As a rule, parent and child are told at the first interview why the child behaves as he does and what the parents do to create or increase his difficulties.

In some cases the first interview is used also to make suggestions for a change in the management of the child. We try to tackle one problem at a time, beginning with the most significant or with one which lends itself to an easy solution. The suggestions are always made as plain and simple as possible, although their execution is never as easy because they involve a change in the existing relationships.

The first suggestion which we invariably make—and which you, the reader, should consider before you try anything else —is to call a truce with the child. This first step is so important that it warrants detailed elaboration and emphasis.

Formerly the child and parent were at war. There must now be a lull in the struggle. It is necessary to convince parents that they must, for the time being, simply let the child go on as he is, being "bad" and making his mistakes. No harm will come of this, as he probably has misbehaved for some time. Meanwhile the parents have to learn to observe the child and themselves—with a better insight into what has been going on. First they must learn to restrain themselves. They must become aware of their tendency to harp repeatedly and learn to stop it. They must start to work on themselves. Many parents claim that they have "tried everything" without success. They generally overlook one possibility: *self-reform*. This is the value of a truce. Without an armistice there can be no peace. And it is their duty, and should be their earnest desire, to make peace with the child. Otherwise, no improvement in the child is possible. By learning to restrain themselves they gradually establish a new relationship between them.

We admit that this first step is the most difficult one. Few parents are able to about-face at once and to arrest their overactivity. If they can, we see results almost at once. In such cases the difficulties may disappear completely after one or two interviews. On the other hand, a slow beginning does not prevent eventual adjustment.

During the ensuing interviews new angles of the problem appear and are discussed. Each time one particular aspect is emphasized. It is necessary to repeat the same explanation and suggestion many times. After all, this is a training process, and training requires systematic repetition. No child will learn to read and write, no person will acquire a skill, by just being informed how to do it. The guidance worker must have as much patience with the parent as the parent must have with himself. If parents are overeager to improve, their anxiety will prevent their adjustment.

According to our experience only a small percentage of parents who seek advice are so deeply disturbed that they require psychotherapy, that is, help in their own emotional adjustment. The great majority require only information and guidance; then they can work out their problems with their children satisfactorily. Their emotional distress, their excitement and irritability, are often the result of their feeling of frustration because they do not know what to do and are nonplussed by the behavior of the child. As they begin to understand and discover different means to meet their problem, they lose their tension, anxiety, and distress. The problems which the child presents cease to be an affliction and become an interesting task, inviting experiment and creativeness. Such an attitude toward a problem situation is imperative, as children will always present problems. Whenever people live together problems exist because all human relationships involve conflicts of interest, clashes of opinion, opposition of desires and temperaments.

The case histories which we shall present are taken from the files of our Chicago Guidance Centers, the psychiatric clinic of the Chicago Medical School, and private practice. While they are similar to some already cited they will better demonstrate the step-by-step procedure. Success or failure depends entirely on the response of the *parents*. We work mostly with the mother; she is the most important person in the child's life, because she influences him more than any other person. If she does not change, accepting and applying our suggestions, the all-important relationship between mother and child remains based on a faulty equilibrium. "Improvement" of the child is by no means limited to the disappearance of certain behavior patterns of which the parents complain. Faulty behavior can be stopped sometimes by direct talks with the child alone; but unless the fundamental equilibrium within the family is changed, no lasting improvement can be expected.

CRYING

Mrs. K. came to the Guidance Center because she was troubled with one specific situation. Her *six-months-old* daughter cried incessantly whenever she was put into her play-pen. Mother tried to ignore the crying, but after some length of time—sometimes after an entire hour—she just couldn't endure it and picked up the baby. What else could she do?

It became evident during a short discussion that both parents were very apprehensive about the welfare, growth, and development of the child. The child cried easily, and the mother especially became upset on such occasions. The baby's eating or sleeping, her weight, her slightest cold or discomfort were important problems and caused considerable concern.

The mother was informed that the atmosphere in which the child grows up is more important than any one single act or event. The child senses the anxiety and apprehension of the mother and has probably already discovered that she can rely on them for getting special attention. She finds it more pleasant to be in mother's arms, to be hugged and cuddled, than to be left by herself in the play-pen. Although mother is careful about what she does, she fails to check her emotions. Her anxiety and sympathy are expressed without words—and the child responds with her own excitement and self-pity.

Consequently, Mrs. K. was advised to leave the child alone in the pen without being afraid that crying will do harm. If she stays in the room, she has to remain completely calm; otherwise, it is preferable that she leave the room.

After one week, Mrs. K. returned and told of her amazement at what happened. The day following her visit to the Center she put the baby back in the pen as usual without saying anything. But this time the baby did not even start to cry at all. For the first time, she quietly accepted being left by herself; and since then, she had not cried when put into her pen.

Mrs. K. realized that it was actually her own attitudes and emotions which had acutely upset the child. The discussion had relieved her anxiety, and the child had sensed it immediately. From that time on, she carefully watched her attitude toward the child, thus altering her whole relationship with her.

FEAR

Gilbert was nine years old when mother came with him for help. He was a fine boy, obedient and kind. But for about a year he had suffered from terrific fears. He had seen his grandfather die, and could not overcome the shock. Since then he had lived in constant fear that something might happen to his parents. He woke up during the night screaming and running to the parents' room to see whether they were all right. He is especially worried about mother. When she leaves the house, he is terror-stricken: something might happen to her. She must call home every hour. If she is five or ten minutes late, he gets frantic. The parents are very sympathetic. They do not fight or scold him, but they don't know what to do with him. Medicines do not quiet him down. Once they sent him to his grandparents' farm. For a few days Gilbert was all right. Then he woke up one night terror-stricken, waking his grandparents. He was convinced that his mother was dying. They had to call home in the middle of the night to reassure him. After that he couldn't stand it there any longer and was sent home.

A short examination of his past development revealed that while he had always been very close to mother, prior to his grandfather's death he had been well-adjusted at home and in school. There were no significant difficulties. He was affectionate and conforming, almost a model child. He even made a good adjustment when a little sister was born three years ago, and was affectionate and friendly toward her. All that had changed when the grandfather died.

At this first interview, no definite conclusion was reached. However, it seemed that the grandfather's death had become important only because of the extreme sympathy and concern which the parents showed about the shock which Gilbert had experienced. The event had occurred at a period in Gilbert's life when he probably felt insecure in the competition with his little sister, who was very cute at that time and attracted considerable attention. Gilbert, not trained for open rebellion and antagonism, undoubtedly capitalized on this new opportunity to gain the limelight and to keep mother even closer to himself than she had been, certainly closer than his age and development would warrant. He was, of course, unaware of this mechanism, as were his parents and other relatives. Mother was advised to stop being impressed by Gilbert's fears; the sympathy which he received only aggravated his condition. But she was also warned that it might take some time to give Gilbert a feeling of independence so that he would not have to resort to his fears.

During his interview, the boy appeared very frank and intelligent, sincere and kind. We had a brief talk with him, asking him first whether he knew why he was so afraid that mother might die. He shook his head. "May we explain it to you?" we asked. He was eager. So we told him that apparently he used his fears to keep his mother concerned with and close to himself, because he might be afraid of losing out to his little sister. Could that be? He grinned with the characteristic "recognition reflex." He had never thought of that before, but he admitted that it might be so. We asked him whether we should, perhaps, help him to overcome this feeling of insecurity. After all, he was a good boy and did not need mother so much any more. He was quite agreeable.

An appointment was made with mother and son for two weeks ahead. A few days before the appointment the mother called to cancel it. Gilbert's fears had completely disappeared.

THE "TEETER-TOTTER" BROTHERS

The following case illustration may be worth mentioning, although no satisfactory results were obtained.

Mrs. D. had difficulties with her son, Tom, aged four. She reported that she became pregnant shortly after Tom was born, and her husband attended to his care. He put Tom to bed, held his hand, and took his part whenever there was an argument. Tom's behavior has become obstreperous. If he does not get his own way, he starts to scream. When he screams mother threatens to shut him in the closet and then he stops. Once, when he started to tease Fred, who is one year younger, she said she would give him an enema if he didn't stop. Mrs. D. uses a stick on both children when they misbehave.

Fred, the younger boy, fights all of Tom's battles. He frequently does cute things and everybody in the family admires him. At nursery school, Fred assumes a protective attitude toward Tom, and tries to console him when he cries.

When the children entered the counsel room, we found to our surprise that Tom was smiling and forward, while Fred trailed behind rather shyly and timidly. Tom answered all the questions, for Fred as well as for himself. Tom had a typical big-brother attitude, was friendly and pleasant, while Fred sat holding to his chair, wriggling and looking very mischievous and taking no part in the conversation.

It was obvious that in the unusual atmosphere of the Guidance Center, the children behaved differently than in the "normal" home and school situations to which they were accustomed. In the trying and embarrassing situation at the counsel room, Tom revealed himself as courageous and friendly toward other people. Apparently Fred was the problem child, contrary to the impression of the mother and teachers. It developed that mother had sided with Fred against the alliance of Tom and his father, thereby placing Fred in a position superior to that of his brother. Left alone to his own resources, Tom might well take care of himself. Under the present circumstances he has no chance to do so, as Fred discourages him and represses him with the approval of mother and teachers.

Mrs. D. was advised not to play one child against the other, or to take sides, but to send both children out of the room if they quarreled or misbehaved. Then she would not be in the position of having to threaten or to spank one or the other.

Two weeks later Mrs. D. reported she had sent both children away from the table when they quarreled, and that they had ceased quarreling at mealtime. She further reported that before the last interview Tom had difficulty in dressing himself in the morning and Fred, the younger one, had helped his older brother to get dressed. However since the interview the circumstances have changed; now Tom dresses himself and Fred seems quite helpless and asks for help. The roles of the two children have reversed completely. Fred, no longer supported against his brother, has lost his temper many times and has also become quite negativistic in nursery school, where he has started to act in a helpless way in regard to dressing.

The children showed the same characteristic behavior as they had previously displayed when brought to the counsel room for their next interview. Fred walked hesitantly into the room, buttoning and unbuttoning his coat as he walked. When Tom entered, he said, "Hello, Fred," walked right over to the chair, and sat down. Then Fred followed and sat down, too. Fred did not answer any questions, completely ignoring them and just playing with his shoes. Fred's interest could be awakened only when he was told to show how well he could unbutton his coat; then his eyes gleamed, and he unbuttoned his coat and took off his coat and hat. Tom, who had been quite responsive up to then, slumped in his chair while Fred was performing and put his fingers in his mouth. When they were ready to leave, Tom again took the lead, stood up and invited Fred to come with him. Fred hesitated, followed slowly, and was coaxed by Tom.

It was explained to Mrs. D. how the children alternately play the baby role, according to which one of them is superior at the moment. Any partiality she shows increases the existing competition. If she wants her children to develop normally, she must establish a different relationship between them, and between herself and them. She was advised to leave the children alone to enjoy each other.

Although Mrs. D. came twice more to the Center, very little

progress was made. It was hard for her to change her attitude and methods, and she did not return to the Center again.

Several points are important in this case. First, the apparent
problem child is not always the real problem; second, the
peculiar and strained situation in the counseling room often
permits a much better evaluation of the existing relationships
than does the "normal" home or school situation; third, progress of one child often leads to regression of his competitor.

Although the mother did not cooperate enough to permit an
adjustment of the children, our brief treatment produced at
least some dynamic changes in the behavior of both children so
that it can be hoped that a new equilibrium will finally result
which will be sounder than the previous one, especially since
the children's teachers realize the nature of the problem and
will manage them accordingly.

THE BULLY

Mrs. P. is a very anxious mother. She describes her difficulties with Robert in great detail; she seems helpless, yet she is
rigid in her own ideas of handling the child.

Robert, age six, has a sister three and a half years old. In her
first interview, mother complains that Robert finds it difficult to make friends, is always alone, does not know what to
do with his time; occasionally he draws, or listens to records.
He bosses other children; sometimes he bribes them and then
suddenly becomes belligerent. He is stubborn. Mother states,
"It is hard to break his will." He cannot get along with anybody, wants his own way, and gets it by devious means.
Mother "has to lick him occasionally." As a small child he was
well behaved. Now he has to be called two or three times in
the morning and he needs assistance in dressing. He eats well,
but swings on his chair, sits on one foot, jumps up and down,
and has to be reminded to sit quietly. He goes to bed only after
much talking and coaxing. He does not put his clothes away.

The interview with Robert shows him as a frank, outspoken

little boy. He thinks mother likes baby more than she likes him. He becomes angry with his sister because she takes his books. He agrees that he wants to be the "big boss." He wants to become a doctor. He likes school and gets along in his class-work, but during recess periods the other children fight and kick him, and he does not know why.

Robert's behavior was interpreted first to him and then to his mother. We explained that Robert believes nobody really loves him, and therefore tries to find his place by demonstrating his power, mainly with his mother. She accepts this provocation and tries to enforce her own rule—without success, of course. Robert becomes convinced that what he needs is power; being liked is the sole privilege of the baby.

The boy understood and accepted our interpretation, which was verified by his "recognition reflex." Mother seemed to be dubious.

Mrs. P. was advised to stop fighting, reminding, coaxing, and punishing. She must win him, give him recognition and responsibility. She must not help him in the morning; that is *his* job and he must take care of himself. At the table, if he does not behave he must be sent away, without sharp words and criticism. Her main task is to improve her relationship with Robert. He does not trust human relationships. The pronounced masculinity of his father probably has some effect on Robert's desire to be "boss," but mother is still the most important factor in his development. Her feeling of helplessness induces her to use violence; although she fails to secure compliance, she stimulates Robert to force her hand.

At the next interview Mrs. P. reported on Robert's progress. He accepts more responsibility; he watches the clock in the morning in order to be in school on time. His table manners have improved considerably after he was sent away once. However, he still cannot play with others, nor by himself.

The boy was as outgoing and frank as he had been during the first interview. He admitted now that he had wanted to bully and boss everybody, including his mother and his school friends. He reported that he had stopped bossing the children, and that they were more friendly toward him.

Mrs. P. was advised to devote some time to playing with Robert—something she had never done before. It was also recommended that she invite other children to the home once a week and provide games for them to play with.

At the third interview, mother reported that Robert had improved considerably. He behaves better, does not resent her requests, is only occasionally disturbing, but sometimes still wants to prove that he can do as he wishes. Once she asked him to put on his galoshes, and he answered, "They are my feet, and I don't mind if they get wet." Mother's efforts to impress him with the consequences of getting sick were naturally unsuccessful. It was explained to her that the point at issue was not the galoshes, but the test of strength. It was less important whether he takes galoshes or not, than to have another contest of power. The mother was defeated because she still tried to impress him with her power of reasoning. The boy had frankly told her, "I am my own boss." He used his power of resistance when she tried to break his rebellion, proving to her *her* helplessness. If the struggle continued, he might even resort to an attitude of revenge. Her playing with him counteracts these tendencies. She herself observed that during their playtime he becomes more cooperative with her.

Mrs. P. reported that Robert is now able to play with children, even with his sister, without attempting to dominate them. The mother is inviting friends to the home. She feels much more relaxed. She stated that she can now keep her domestic help who previously had refused to stay because of Robert.

At the next interview, the question of Robert's going to bed came up. It takes considerable coaxing to get him to bed on time. He gets out of bed several times before he finally goes to sleep; sometimes he disturbs his parents during the night. Mrs. P. has contemplated possible natural consequences and reasoned that if Robert is so thoughtless about the parents' rest, they, too, should wake him up from his sleep!—an indication of how she still believes in retaliation, in the principle of "an eye for an eye." It was suggested to her that she find better and more logical consequences. She could make an agreement with Robert about the number of hours' sleep he needs; he would know at what time he should be in bed. Then she should watch *without saying one word*. If he is not in bed on time, he has to make up the sleep next evening by going to bed as many hours earlier as it took him to get to bed the night before. (It is advisable to let older children make up the lost time on *Saturday*, which may mean no dinner, no movies—depending on the amount of sleep lost during the week.)

The last interview showed marked improvement, not only in Robert's behavior, but in his relationship with his mother. Both are much happier. His going to bed is no longer a problem. He takes care of himself. He stopped indulging in temper displays after mother walked out of the house during one of his tantrums. He no longer tries to dominate her as she neither bosses nor pushes him around. He and mother play together and enjoy each other. His relationship with other children is much better. He likes to play with them. He is convinced now that he is liked by children and loved by his parents.

Robert's drive for power was inspired by his mother's attitude. First, she was overprotective and anxious, and when the situation became complicated, especially after the birth of the second child, when Robert felt left out, then she became rigid and punitive. Each recommendation made to her was directed toward changing their relationship. The changes in Robert's attitude toward mother—and hers toward him—were then reflected in the changed behavior of Robert outside of the house. Robert responded immediately to the interpretation, and mother was able to realize her errors and to adopt new methods. For this reason the adjustment of both was exceptionally fast.

THE BABY TYRANT

Joe W., nine years old, was referred to the psychiatric clinic after passing through several other departments, because his overweight resisted all dietary and glandular treatment. Apparently, Mrs. W. was unable to control the food intake of the boy.

The mother reported that Joe does not maintain his diet. When he comes home from school he is hungry and asks for food. She reminds him that he should not eat between meals, but he goes to the pantry and takes what he wants. If she tries to stop him, he becomes furious, so she gives in. "After all, he is really hungry." Every day she has long talks with him about the need to control himself, but he is so hungry that he cannot refrain from eating more.

However, the difficulties which he causes are not only in regard to eating. He wets the bed. He is constantly around his mother. If she goes out, he is afraid she will not come home on time. When she leaves the house she has to tell him where she goes and when she expects to return. She plans her shopping trips so that she will be home before he returns from school. If she should be a few minutes late, he stands in front of the house and publicly makes a scene.

Another area of conflict is the radio. He listens to it as long as he likes to. He refuses to go to bed on time, goes only when the parents retire. He occasionally requires help in undressing and washing. He dresses himself in the morning, but does not lace his shoes. He cannot tie them. "Perhaps he is too fat for it," is mother's comment.

He is doing all right in school, but cannot get along with the children in the neighborhood. They are rough and gang up on him because he is Italian and they are Irish. They do damage to the neighborhood. Therefore, mother tells him that they are not the right company for him. He has one boy friend who is a little older but very dull and does everything Joe wants. When children visit him, he does not let them touch his toys because "they might spoil them." He takes a circuitous route on his way to school to avoid the other children of his neighborhood.

Joe has a brother who is twelve years older than he. He fights with him and feels that the brother tries to boss him. The brother becomes angry if Joe misbehaves or does not obey. Joe is jealous whenever his brother gets more than he or does what he is unable to do.

Summary: Joe is an overprotected child who dominates his mother and wants his way as compensation for being the youngest and smallest in the family. His excessive craving for food is his weapon to defeat his mother, as are his bed-wetting, his refusal to dress himself completely, his ascendancy in regard to radio and going to bed, and his control of mother's activities. His difficulties with children are the consequence of his desire to dominate and his refusal to participate on equal terms. Mother keeps him too close to herself and does not know how to manage him, fighting and giving in at the same time. The efforts of mother and brother to overpower him meet with the child's increased determination to overpower them.

The situation was explained to both mother and boy, who seemed to understand the interpretation. The boy acknowledged with the "recognition reflex" the suggestion that he might want to be the boss. Mother was advised to act rather than to argue. She should stop her talk about food but see to it that Joe ate nothing between meals; she should stop tying his shoelaces, and should turn off the radio at 9 P.M. If she would relinquish her fear and concern about him, he would learn to take care of himself. If she refused to succumb to his domination, he could not continue it. It is unnecessary to report to him where she is going and when she will return, or be on hand invariably when he gets home; he can assume responsibility for himself. Mother said she would carry out our recommendations.

Two weeks later Mrs. W. reported that the brother had shown Joe how to tie his shoelaces, and Joe has tied them ever since. Mrs. W. has given him a key to the apartment, and he goes in when mother is absent and tends to his own needs. He now goes to bed at 9 P.M. except on one night a week when he is permitted to listen to one radio show. There is no argument about eating; he is given a little food after school occasionally; then he goes out to play. He has made friends with another boy. The principal remaining problem is his bed-wetting. He sleeps with his older brother, and they quarrel because of Joe's bed-wetting.

During the interview, Joe spoke little, looking away when addressed, but his facial expression and "reflex" reaction showed that he understood and agreed. We had a long discussion with him without his saying a word: his facial expressions indicated his responses. Asked whether he wanted, perhaps, to punish his brother by bed-wetting, because he felt bossed and pushed around by him, he answered positively with the "reflex."

This time Mrs. W. was advised merely to continue the diet and not to mention the bed-wetting. We wanted to see whether our discussion with the boy about this subject would have any effect.

Two weeks later: Joe gets along well. He ties his shoes. He no longer quarrels with mother if she is not home on time or refuses to tell him where she goes. In his relationships with other children, he still prefers his old friend whom he can boss. He is wetting his bed only two or three times a week, rather than nightly as he had been doing.

It was explained to Mrs. W. that Joe's improvement in regard to bed-wetting indicated that our explanation was probably correct and that she should stay out of this conflict between the brothers. However, she should try not to baby Joe and should so instruct his brother. Joe was more vocal during this interview.

Two weeks later: Joe dresses himself and goes to school punctually without coaxing; he enters the home with his own key. There have been no arguments with mother about either homecoming, radio, or food. He wet the bed only twice in two weeks.

Two weeks later: Bed-wetting has stopped altogether. Joe behaves well, is in bed generally at 8:30, dresses and undresses himself alone, goes in and out of the house, makes less fuss about the food.

A new problem has arisen—Joe refuses to do his homework. Mother was advised to explain to him, without pleading or constant reminding, that he could not listen to the radio before he has finished his homework. Joe has dropped his old boy friend and turned to a new one who is much more his equal.

Two weeks later: Joe has wet the bed once. However, his homework is done every day. He has lost three pounds during the past two weeks. He gets along much better, not only with mother but also with children. He now plays with the Irish boys on the playground without complaining.

Two weeks later: No bed-wetting at all. Joe passed his school work with improved marks. He gets along well with children, has new friends. At home there is peace and order, no radio problem any more. Mother and Joe are happy over the improvement in their relationship. Case closed.

Joe's case is similar to the previous case of Robert. Here again the child and the mother caught on rather quickly to the interpretations of their mutual mistakes and began their reorientation immediately after the first interview. In this case, one has the feeling that the achieved adjustment had solved the immediate problems of the boy and certainly changed the mother-child relationship; but the peculiar position of the boy in the family set-up and a certain rigidity in both mother and child may lead to new complications whenever a new task finds them unprepared. In such a case each may revert to his old schemes.

THE "HOLY TERROR"

Mrs. L. brought eight-year-old Mike to the Guidance Center without an appointment. She wanted immediate help and was unable to accept our request that she first make an appointment with the social worker who would take the history and background of the case. She remained in the counsel room, constantly causing disturbance either by running to the social worker for more information about the appointment or interrupting the discussion of another case by loudly asking the psychiatrist when he thought he could see her. Mike had been sent home from school the day before because he had jerks and convulsions. The teacher thought he had St. Vitus's dance.

At the appointed interview with mother and grandmother, we were informed that Mike had had tics for about two months, jerking his head, sniffling, clearing his throat, and, more recently, shaking his whole body rather violently.

Mother and father are seldom home and Mike is under the care of his maternal grandparents. There is a baby sister who is six and a half months old. All members of the family criticize each other in front of him. He can dress himself but refuses, so mother, rather than argue with him, dresses him. At the table he uses his fingers instead of his knife and fork, and messes up the floor. He refuses to eat anything but meat, and so he is constantly nagged at the table. He does not help around the house and is destructive. Children do not want to play with him because he hits them. He takes things away from others. He calls mother as if he were in great trouble; she runs to him in panic, and then he laughs and asks if he has worried her. The worst trouble is getting him to bed. Until last year mother had to wipe him after each bowel movement. She "cured" him by smearing the excreta on his face. Mother hits him frequently and nags him constantly. Mr. L. is stern and just sends him out. He scares Mike. Father holds mother responsible for the boy's behavior, and the parents are considering breaking up their marriage on these grounds. Both grandparents are extremely apprehensive; they overindulge Mike and always side with him.

Mike loves school and has good grades, but is rated poorly on self-control and courtesy. He talks out of turn, is destructive, and does not pay attention. One day he was sent home from school as a "punishment" for his tic.

Mother and grandparents are extremely alarmed about his present "nervous condition" and want immediate help. He has been given bromides and barbiturates for two months, but the condition has become worse. During the interview they repeatedly asked, "What can we do, what shall we do?" without waiting for any suggestions; when a suggestion was offered they immediately argued against it and refused to accept any advice, sometimes taking a stand against each other. The whole interview showed the family atmosphere—apprehension, excitement, conflict, and disorder.

The boy was very frank and outspoken during his interview. His body shook violently but his movements were not choreatic (typical for St. Vitus's dance). Asked why he trembled, he answered, "Shall I tell you why I do this? [jerking his head] Really something in my head tells me, 'Do it, do it.'" To another question he replied, "If you think I am jealous of sister— I ain't. They [the family] tell me this. I don't mind if they are busy with sister. I just go to my room and read comics." It was explained to him that his pride probably prevents him from admitting his jealousy, but that because of it he tries new and more potent tricks to make his family become more concerned with him. He wants to be the "boss" and the "baby" at the same time. While watching his jerking, we were impressed with the suddenness and vigor (drama?) of the movements. So we ventured a guess. Could it be that he used these mannerisms to frighten and impress mother and grandparents even more than he does with his other acts? He responded with the "recognition reflex." Then we demonstrated while talking to him, how terrifying such a sudden jerking movement is. He too, was startled—and smiled. Our discussion then ended.

We explained to mother and grandmother that Mike could not be helped until the whole home situation is changed. Before we could give advice, the fighting and bickering, arguing and attentiveness to Mike must stop. We assured them that Mike was not suffering from St. Vitus's dance; his symptoms were only his way of impressing them and getting more attention. Mother and grandmother declared their extreme eagerness to work out their problems with us and to come again next week.

We have not seen them again. When mother telephoned to break the next appointment, she overflowed with expressions of gratitude. Mike had stopped jerking the day after the interview, and had not twitched since. But he had started to swear, using terrible words. Mother broke the two following appointments with one excuse or another—and is still grateful that Mike does not jerk any more. Apparently that was all she was interested in.

COMPULSIVE NEUROSIS

The development of a severe neurosis in young children is a rare occurrence. The case cited herein demonstrates that the severity of the symptoms in children does not have the same significance as similar symptoms have in adults whose treatment is generally very difficult and long.

During the first interview the following history was taken. Eight-year-old Sharon had been a "normal," healthy child until one month ago. She had been a charming, obedient, and kind little girl who performed equally well in school and at home. Suddenly she developed fears of blindness, of infantile paralysis, and of diphtheria. She could not breathe and was terrified of death. She repeatedly asked mother whether she would die or become sick, demanding reassurance and sympathy. For the last four days she had been afraid her food was poisoned, and mother had to taste all foods before she would eat. She drooled because she could not swallow her saliva, fearing the germs in it. She lived in constant expectation of disaster. She had many compulsive symptoms, counted the steps or other objects when she walked on the streets, and developed new symptoms each day. When she was not concerned about her symptoms she was impertinent, mocked her mother if scolded, and demanded continual reassurance that she was loved. One day she pointed a knife at her mother and on another occasion threw a ball violently at her parents when they were together. The parents always carefully avoided any demonstration of affection between them in the child's presence. At school, however, Sharon behaved well, was exceptionally advanced for her age, was liked by the children and played with them.

Past history: Three years ago Sharon had an episode of disturbance when she enrolled in school. She did not want to leave mother, was afraid mother would not be home when she came back from school. Mother had to go through a ritual of promising that she would be home, crossing her heart and repeating the same assurance many times. The child was taken to a psychiatrist who arranged play therapy for her once a week. She went for nine months and was completely well when discharged.

Her parents had been divorced when the child was two and a half years old. Since then, until recently, patient had lived alone with her mother. They were constantly together although the mother had remarried three years ago. But her second husband had been in the service and returned only two and a half months before mother and daughter came to us.

During the interview with the child, she maintained that she was happy, not at all sick, and she denied any fears. She said she did not need or want help. She denied ever having seen another doctor but spoke of a playroom in a hospital, of drawing pictures and eating candy. Upon further insistence she stated she did not want to talk, that she did not like the doctor, and stalked from the room.

The following impression was related to the mother at the first interview. It seemed that Sharon had been completely dependent on mother and wanted to possess her exclusively. Her first disturbance, three years ago, was directed against her mother's remarriage, but mainly against entering school. Apparently the play therapy induced her to accept temporary separation from mother and prepared her for school. The present episode seemed to be caused by the return of her stepfather, and by her fear of losing her monopoly on mother. Her symptoms were the expression of her rebellion and were her tools to occupy mother constantly, not only forcing uninterrupted attention, but also concern and worry. Normally, she never was openly rebellious and seemingly wanted to please mother and be a good girl. Now she could neither admit to herself her rebellion and opposition nor express them without the excuse of being sick. Furthermore, we suspected from her symptoms that the girl had been subjected to much subtle pressure. Behind the mutual closeness and affection existed a contest of power between two determined females.

Mother was perplexed about this explanation. She stated that her husband had expressed similar ideas about Sharon's using her symptoms coercively, but she had not accepted his explanation. However, now she could see that our impression might be correct.

She was advised to ignore the girl's behavior, though this treatment would probably increase Sharon's violence and symptoms. However, mother should not permit herself to be intimidated or dominated by the child's behavior. On the other hand, she should not become angry or impatient, should not show annoyance, but should be affectionate and play with the child. As a first step she would have to overcome her own apprehension and distress and would have to establish a new relationship with the child.

Three days later mother reported the following development. She was capable of maintaining an attitude of neutrality. The girl first pleaded, then raved, then attacked her with scissors and with a knife. She wrote on the walls, "Mother is a stinker." She was destructive, cut mother's nylons, and threw objects around. She begged mother to kiss her when she was in bed, to keep her, Sharon, from falling asleep as she was afraid of her dreams. Mother told her she was willing to kiss her because she loved her, but not after she had been bidden good night. Last night she wanted to get into mother's bed because she had been alarmed by a fire siren, but mother refused and the girl went to sleep on the floor. When mother paid no attention she got up in half an hour, asked for a phenobarbital, and retired to her own bed without any coaxing or other persuasion.

Sharon had expressed her anger at us to her mother and had protested that we had changed mother's personality. She asked mother why she did not get angry when she was destructive. She said, "I don't know what makes me so bad. God didn't make me like this. How can I be good?" Her mother advised her to talk it over with us. Sharon did not want to go to school.

We commended the mother for her attitude and for her ability to retain her composure in the face of the child's provocative behavior. She was advised to continue in the same way.

Mother came one week later to report that Sharon was recovering from a mild case of measles. Prior to her illness, her aggressiveness had subsided; now, in her convalescence, she again had become openly hostile, kicking mother and others. Her compulsions also had increased; she counted steps and spat her retained saliva on the floor. She placed an ashtray on mother's head when mother was seated; went into the parents' room after they had retired, turning on the lights; followed her mother everywhere about the house, wanting to hold her hand. Sharon was now afraid of contracting polio and, if mother was not with her all the time, was fearful lest she die in mother's absence. She did not want to listen to the radio because she might acquire new fears. Her eating habits also changed. After our first consultation Sharon had determined not to eat the same food as the parents but to have something special. Now she decided to take nothing but milk. On the other hand, she had asked mother to have me telephone her at home because she wanted help to overcome her worries.

At the next interview Sharon was willing to talk about her problems. She was quiet, friendly, cooperative, and attentive. An attempt was made to give her some understanding of the unconscious reasons behind her behavior—that she was accustomed to having mother to herself and had rebelled against her father's return because she did not want to share mother with father; that she used her fears to make mother become concerned about her; that she was angry with mother and annoyed both parents to punish them and to gain attention. Sharon listened attentively and responded several times with the "recognition reflex."

The next week the stepfather accompanied Sharon to our office because mother was sick. He reported much improvement. Sharon lost her temper only once a day. She continued, however, to swear at mother and father and to expectorate all over the house. She went for a ride with her girl friend, leaving the house without her parents for the first time. It was still difficult to get her out of the house to play with children; she generally followed mother from room to room. She ate better and did not demand that her food be tasted. For the first time she went to bed by herself without fussing.

The next interview with the mother, a few days later, indicated additional progress. Mother had learned to let Sharon experience the consequences of her actions. If Sharon became angry, mother simply left the room; when she returned, the girl generally was quiet and conformed to the necessary rules of order. Previously the selection of the daily wardrobe had been a major problem. Now, after a short discussion between mother and Sharon in which mother expressed her opinion but left the decision to Sharon, Sharon accepted mother's choice without remonstrance. When mother succumbed to a temptation to coax her, Sharon stopped her, saying, "That is none of your affair." Mother did not feel hurt, but smiled inwardly;

she recognized now how much pressure she had exerted before. It was still difficult for her at times to restrain herself; but she accepted increasingly her new role and relationship and no longer became upset by the child's coercive activity which she now recognized as a reflection of the forcefulness she had previously exerted. When Sharon started to demand reassurance about her symptoms and fears, mother referred her to the doctor and encouraged Sharon to seek advice there. (The previous evening Sharon had actually telephoned us and asked what she could do about her fears. Our answer was a reference to their purpose, that she wanted to absorb her mother's attention by demanding sympathy, consolation, and reassurance. She was praised for her cleverness in achieving her end, and told to continue her methods.[2] The girl seemed to be satisfied with the answer—sic!—and ended the call with friendly thanks.)

The principal remaining difficulty at the next interview was the girl's "inability" to swallow her saliva. The problem was discussed with Sharon. She volunteered the information during the discussion that she was bad and did not deserve to be happy. It was pointed out to her that one of the reasons for not swallowing the saliva was that she considered everything in herself to be bad, including her saliva, which she fancied was full of germs. She also was angry with her present situation, and expectorating was an emotional expression of her dissatisfaction and contempt for order and regulation, particularly since she no longer manifested her anger overtly through her temper tantrums.

During the discussion with mother a policy was established in regard to Sharon's expectorating. Mother was to tell her that she should go up to her own room if she wanted to expectorate on the floor instead of using the appropriate receptacle.

Two weeks later, the mother reported that the expectorating had stopped. Mother and daughter spent much time play-

---

[2] Such "anti-suggestion" is often very effective. Children seldom take such remarks as sarcastic, because they recognize what is meant.

ing together and there was little disturbance in the home. Only once during this period had a relapse occurred, shortly after Sharon had visited her own father. After this visit she berated her mother and struck at her several times. (Apparently the girl was unable to forgive her mother for having remarried instead of devoting the rest of her life exclusively to her!) Sharon did not like to have her hair combed and sometimes became angry on such occasions. (The rebellion against being overpowered or handled.)

During the next few weeks the child occasionally became moody as an appeal to mother for special consideration. Occasionally she struck mother who managed to ignore the abuse composedly.

After three months of treatment the case was closed as "recovered." She became "her old self" but on a different equilibrium with mother. Several months later, during a casual encounter, mother reported that Sharon had continued well and happy without a recurrence of any difficulties.

MENTAL RETARDATION

Geraldine at the age of seven behaves like a baby. She can neither dress nor undress herself; occasionally she rips her clothing when she tries to undress and gets angry at her inability to do so. She does not make any attempt to dress herself. She frequently loses her temper and kicks her parents if they do not give in. She does not go to bed by herself; mother has to lie down with her, or she will not fall asleep. During the night, she calls her parents frequently, and they always respond and quiet her. She started to talk at the age of five; her speech is unintelligible and guttural. She will not talk at all to strangers. The parents make her repeat each word to improve her enunciation. At the table she has to be fed, and mother must tell her stories or else she will not eat. She was entered in a parochial school at the age of five, but has recently been transferred to a public school, where she has been placed in an ungraded room. There she refuses to talk to the teacher and does not play with the children.

The school authorities informed the mother shortly before she came to the Center that they could not keep the girl, whom they considered mentally retarded, and advised the parents to send the child to a state institution for the feeble-minded. The parents were horrified at the prospect. They asked for postponement of the decision in order to seek psychiatric help. Although the teacher expressed doubt as to the possibility of any improvement, the parents pleaded and gained respite.

Geraldine is an only child and has had many serious illnesses during her childhood. The parents admit they have spoiled and overprotected her. At the interview Geraldine was completely passive and unresponsive.

The parents were told that it was impossible to make a diagnosis at the first interview. The child might be feeble-minded —but we felt unable to determine the extent of her mental deficiency so long as the parents did not give her a chance to develop her abilities. They would first have to change their approach to her. Geraldine must no longer be permitted to put them completely into her service. They must encourage her to act for herself. Since everything was done for her, there was no need for Geraldine to make any effort; she received too much by not functioning. Both parents were kind and sincere, although they admitted that they occasionally spanked the child when they did not know how to handle her, particularly when she threw a temper tantrum.

The parents understood our explanations fully. For the first time the child's behavior began to make sense to them. They expressed their willingness to cooperate in any way. During the first interview we offered more recommendations than we generally dare to give at this early stage, because the parents seemed to be ready for specific help. They were advised (1) to let the child go to bed alone in a separate room, to pay no attention to whatever she might do, and not to respond to any call during the night; (2) to leave the child alone when she had a fit of temper; (3) to disregard her bad speech, to stop making her repeat words, but, on the other hand, to ignore her when she speaks unintelligibly; (4) to play with her and to show her much affection, substituting this affection and play for the previous services to the child; (5) to stop scolding, nagging, coaxing, and spanking, but to remain calm whatever the child might do.

Two weeks later parents and child came again, reporting definite progress. The parents seemed to be much encouraged. Geraldine speaks more plainly; she goes to bed earlier and by herself; there is no longer any fussing; she undresses herself, although she still has difficulties in dressing; she and her parents play together, and whatever has to be done is discussed and agreed upon in advance. Geraldine asked them once why they no longer scolded or punished her; she expressed openly her surprise at this change.

This time the parents were counseled to let the child eat by herself and to send her away from the table if she threw her food around.

Two weeks later, the mother said that Geraldine is doing much more for herself; she now feeds herself and eats well. Her sleeping habits are very good. She goes to bed early and stays in bed. In the morning she arises upon being awakened, without having to be called or reminded. She talks much more, no longer mumbles, and her enunciation is much better and clearer. She can almost dress herself completely. She plays with blocks, with a ball, and with a xylophone, and wants to play with daddy. She expresses a desire to see her cousin. She does not mind if mother leaves her alone in the room. There are no more tantrums, no kickings, since parents ignore them completely. They, on their side, never scold or spank any more, are very careful never to raise their voices. Child and parents are happier than ever before. The one remaining difficulty is Geraldine's objection to having her hair combed, but mother is confident that she can overcome this obstacle, too.

The situation in school has already changed. Geraldine is

more friendly with the children and likes to play with them. She also talks freely with them. A few weeks ago the teacher had urged the removal of the child as a hopeless case, considering her moronic and "deaf." During the last week, the teacher has recognized and admitted the progress Geraldine has made, and is now cooperative in helping with the child's development. There is no longer any talk of removal and commitment.

The case was dismissed after three interviews. A final judgment of the child's mental ability has been postponed until the child has been given more time to develop.

PSEUDO-FEEBLE-MINDEDNESS

Rick was four years old when his parents brought him to the Guidance Center to find out whether anything could be done for his development. He sat quietly between father and mother, leaning toward and holding onto his father with a sweet expression on his face. He did not respond to any questions, keeping his face blank and eventually turning himself away. He muttered something which was interpreted by his parents as "Go home."

The parents told of several severe operations which the child had undergone. They were in constant fear for the life of their only child and watched over him carefully. He started to walk at eighteen months, having been sick before. He has never learned to talk, nor does he listen. He cannot do anything, not even control his bladder. He is completely dependent on his parents. The parents had taken him previously for psychiatric and psychological examination. According to the mental test the boy *was diagnosed as feeble-minded and deaf-mute*. However, the parents had observed some reactions which may indicate that he is able to hear, at least some sounds.

It was evident that at the present time no decision could be made about Rick's mental condition and possible development because he was so overprotected. Therefore, the parents were advised to stop their overanxiety and apprehension, to let him alone and not be so much occupied with him. Whether he could hear and talk could be ascertained only after he had experienced that not talking or listening no longer produced the desired results. No other problem of Rick was discussed at this time.

At the next interview mother reported that, to their surprise, Rick had stopped bed-wetting during the night. She wanted to know now how to make him eat properly. He grabs the food at the table by the handful and stuffs it into his mouth. Mother was advised to give him a spoon to eat with, and if he refuses to use it, to take his plate away. We were informed that Rick becomes angry and agitated if he does not get what he wants, and the parents have tried up to now to upset him as little as possible. We pointed out that Rick has to learn that his anger will not produce results. The only way to teach him this is to leave the room whenever he gets angry; her mood, however, must not be unhappy or oversolicitous.

At this session Rick refused to go into the playroom with the other children, but stayed with his mother. He was somewhat restless, although he behaved rather well. This time he did not indicate a desire to go home.

The third week Rick showed further improvement. He had wet his bed but once, *after* he had awakened (as if to show that he still needs more care and attention). But he had learned to speak some words. Mother had refused to do things for him when he just pointed; so he started to name what he wanted. Mother had to be cautioned against urging him to speak plainly, which she had started to do. That is undue attention. She also had hesitated to take the food away when Rick did not use the spoon. Instead of applying the logical consequences, the parents had tried unsuccessfully to "teach him to eat with a spoon." Obviously, it was difficult for them to lose their concern and sympathy. It was pointed out to them that Rick needs to be encouraged and not to be served.

At the next session we heard of Rick's new trick to keep

mother's attention. Instead of wetting his bed, he asked several times during the night to be taken to the bathroom. His vocabulary increased, but he developed a new way of demonstrating that he was not listening: he turned his head away. He showed greater obedience to his father who is not home as much and does not give in so easily as mother. Rick now gets attention by stalling at bedtime and refusing to fall asleep until late. These new attention-getting mechanisms were explained to mother; she was told not to be deceived by such efforts. It is better to let him be awake until he is tired enough to fall asleep than to make a fuss or comment. He should be put on the toilet before he goes to bed, but under no circumstances should he be taken to the bathroom during the night; he must learn to control his bladder. So far Rick had not learned to exert himself in any direction.

The next week, according to the mother, was peaceful and happy. Rick did not wet his bed or ask for the toilet. He talked more and started to play with other children. His tantrums ceased. He was put to bed on time and fell asleep shortly after. Mother felt quite encouraged.

Rick still gave the impression of a very retarded child. At four he behaved liked a two-year-old. But for the first time he went to the playroom in the Center, starting to play by putting blocks one after the other to "build a train." He came into the counsel room, climbed clumsily on the bench, looking around for help. When he was not helped, he managed to get up by himself. However, he soon put himself in a precarious position, giving the impression that he would fall off at any moment, apparently to induce help and attention. He almost did fall—but, as nobody helped, he immediately regained control of himself and landed on his feet. He seemed to have discovered "poor muscle coordination" as a means of getting attention and service, but, if neither were given, he could take care of himself very well. He was very orderly in his play, showed a remarkable interest in minute details, such as examining tiny things like a hair, a blade of grass, a spider's web, or by drawing tiny figures in orderly arrangement. This seemed to indicate a rather well-developed intelligence.

At this point mother was advised to play with him a great deal.

After two weeks Rick's speech has improved further. He now uses not only nouns but also pronouns. Once he came to his mother and said, "I lost my mittens." When he was given salad, he said, "This is good." There is no longer the slightest question about his ability to hear. He sings some songs which he hears on the radio. He is beginning to dress himself.

This time he cried when brought to the counsel room. He refused to sit down or to pay any attention to what was said to him. Apparently he realized that his devices for extracting assistance were not effective here. One of his new tricks was to let his mother wait on the street while he followed her very slowly. Mother had to be reminded not to coax and urge him. She could ask him whether he wanted to come along or whether she should proceed by herself. Perhaps he could show her the way home? There was evidence that Rick still tried to run the show by making subtle demands on his mother to which she submitted, as usual.

This time Rick did not play with the children in the playroom but watched them from a distance.

Next week mother told us that Rick has begun to pick up his toys at night and to wash his hands and face. He also tries to put on his shoes and stockings. Nevertheless, he does occasionally become infantile and makes funny noises. He leans on his mother whenever he can. He dawdles, and mother finds it hard to refrain from reminding him; most of the time she merely watches him and he notices and seems to enjoy it. His table manners are much better since his food is taken away when he does not eat properly. On the street mother did try hiding around the corner when Rick refused to leave another boy to go home with her, and Rick has come promptly ever since.

At this session, Rick played contentedly in the playroom.

Mother has to be reminded again neither to help nor to direct Rick; instead of calling his attention to the consequences by reminding him of them, she must apply them without any further comment.

A month elapsed before the next visit to the Center. Rick has been getting along fine physically, his mother reported. He wets his bed rarely. He has started to go to nursery school and likes it very much. His teacher is satisfied, although he does not play much with other children.[3] He does not cry; he plays alone with blocks or builds long straight lines of trains. He does not always hear—or better, heed—what people say. During the nap period, he is restless and talks to himself. At lunch he first refused to ask for his dessert, but finally said, "Cake."

Rick came happily into the counsel room for his interview and talked to several people although his speech was not very clear. He was cheerful and pleasant and unafraid. He climbed on the bench and sat quietly. However, he did not respond when talked to and pretended not to hear. When we snapped a finger before his face, he assumed a blank expression, staring beyond us as if he could neither hear nor see; but after a while he tried to make a similar motion with his own fingers. His manner throughout the interview was haughty and oblivious of what was going on around him.

This session was also attended by Rick's nursery-school teacher. She was advised to let other children work with Rick when he built trains and to encourage him to participate in simple organized games. If he disturbed the other children during the rest period, his bed should be put in a separate room without scolding or fuss, and he should be permitted to come back when he was willing to be quiet.

Mother came again next week. She reported that Rick has discovered and enjoys colors. He goes around the house picking out all the blue objects, saying, "Blue," and does the same

[3] We did not attempt to give another psychological test because of the possible discouraging effect of another low I.Q.

with other colors. His speech is improving steadily. He can repeat the whole story of the "Three Little Pigs." He likes to set up his toy soldiers in marching formation.

During the interview Rick named all the colors and obviously enjoyed doing so. He counted his fingers, but refused to tell the story of the "Three Little Pigs."

Two weeks later, mother reported briefly that things were going well and she had no special problems. She is working now, and the family seems to be adjusting satisfactorily.

A week later: Rick has just recovered from a cold. During his illness he was inclined to whine and cry and to revert to his baby ways. He plays with blocks and does a lot of careful building, picking up his blocks when he is through playing with them. He likes to listen to stories. His speech is improving. A year ago he did not utter a word, a few months ago he said a number of single words, and now he is able to talk in sentences. He puts on his own shoes. At the interview he was very friendly, played with a pencil, and told what he was doing.

During the next few weeks, he had several colds, which threw him back somewhat in his behavior. However, he now learns very quickly, enjoys colors, numbers, and the alphabet, and knows all the letters. He is improving rapidly socially. He takes special delight in colors and he uses them as a social game to amuse guests. He designates all the people he knows by a color. His mother is "Red Mama," father is "Yellow Daddy," he himself is "Blue Rick." Relatives are "Pink Grace," "Purple Gertrude," and "Green Bessie." Young children are usually "white," older ones "orange." His grandparents are "Orange." This designation as colors is not done haphazardly. He always connects the same person with the same color. Apparently Rick associates emotions with color. At this interview he was very proud to mention the "colors" of the various persons present. He seems to use this particular stratagem to impress people and to gain special attention thereby.

In the nursery school he is not as cooperative as the other

children, but nevertheless is participating. Once he clumsily disturbed a game, and the other children refused to play with him. He became angry and knocked all the toys down. For the first time he was active and aggressive, and, in his case, this can be considered as progress. He plays nicely with a younger cousin. He is becoming a little more cooperative and sociable. However, since he quarreled with the children at school, he has shown a little reluctance to return to kindergarten. He sings the songs he learns at nursery school, but sometimes his words are still indistinct.

When he is ready to leave school he puts on his wraps alone, unless his mother is present; then he insists on help. Rick is generally amiable and occasionally a little boisterous. He has a one-track mind, and when he becomes interested in any one thing, he refuses to be diverted. He assumes a blank, stolid expression as if he could not see or hear what has been suggested, and willfully concentrates only on what he has in mind. Taken to the zoo, his interest seemed to be in the people rather than in the animals, at which he hardly looked. However, when he reached home, he pointed out the animals in his picture book, naming them and the parts of their bodies. "This is a lion, and this is his tail."

During the interview Rick refused to sit on the bench, but walked around the table and leaned against the social worker, lifting his arms as if he wanted to be picked up. He did not answer questions until asked about colors. He counted to twelve, counted his own fingers, and named the printed letters of the alphabet. But no response could be drawn from him on any other subject; he merely looked blank when anything else was mentioned.

Mother was advised that if Rick does not want to dress for school, she should assume that he is ill and put him to bed, giving him no toys and feeding him only liquids. Her manner should be kind and gentle, but firm. She was told, however, not to attempt it if she were doubtful of this procedure and of her ability to execute it without being tense and nervous.

The next report of the schoolteacher indicated that Rick is beginning to reach out to the group and to recede from his isolation. He got into a fight again. He is still somewhat backward in putting on his jacket and heavy pants. He makes friends with other children outside of school. He has not wet his bed for a long time. The mother was advised to be more careful not to help him dress, and it was suggested that she invite children to the home to play with Rick. Apparently the mother still gets angry with him sometimes, but she tries to do or say nothing on these occasions. Rick, too, loses his temper from time to time.

Whenever he is sick, it takes Rick a little time to readjust to school. On the street he greets acquaintances in a smiling manner. At times he still refuses to talk and assumes a remote look, but usually he smiles gaily when spoken to. Occasionally he will pretend not to hear. He is much happier than he has ever been, but is inclined not to trust everybody. Sometimes he antagonizes children and withdraws from the group, but most of the time he participates and cooperates.

At this session, Rick drew figures with neat, quick strokes and printed letters with both hands, shifting the pencil or crayon frequently from one hand to the other.

A few months later he became somewhat contrary after a period of respiratory disorders. He gets along beautifully with children younger than himself. He likes to teach, but cries when other children reject him. He sometimes acts tough, "I am going to beat you up—I am going to hit you." Mother still wavers between a growing anger and oversympathy if he misbehaves. Although she has learned much, she is not always as firm and objective with Rick as she should be.

During one interview he first sat down among the parents, pretending not to hear what was said to him. But then he came up to the bench, showed a drawing, and described what he did. He still has his own way, doing what he wants and rejecting what he dislikes, refusing to stop what he is doing. But he smiles all the time. When he was told that the interview was over, he pretended not to hear and went on writing. The teacher said that on some days he is more sociable than on others. Generally he is very cooperative when asked to do things.

In the playroom Rick colored rather rapidly and in a short time asked for several sheets of paper. He drew a picture of a train with flag, bell, smokestack, and many wheels on the engine.

After one and a half years' attendance at the Guidance Center, Rick had made real progress. Our prognosis was that an adequate adjustment could be expected eventually, although certain defects on the intellectual plane might remain. Both parents were cooperative and intelligent in the handling of the child and showed considerable insight, although their own emotional reaction was sometimes inadequate.

One year later, at the age of seven, Rick entered public school. His grades were all "Excellent," without any check for any particular difficulty. He is a charming, cooperative boy, but sometimes still displays a peculiar attitude of remoteness and aloofness. Then he looks like a prince who surveys the world around him. His overall adjustment, however, has been satisfactory. The latest information we have indicates that the boy is now far ahead of his class and the school is considering a double promotion.

This case is important for many reasons. It demonstrates first how wrong it is to be influenced by a first impression if the situation appears hopeless. Pessimism is never justifiable, as one can never really know how the situation will develop if the parents learn to deal with the problem more adequately. For this reason an early repetition of the first I.Q. test was omitted, as it would only have had discouraging effects on the parents and the child. At that time we could not know what became apparent later on—that the child was not retarded but actually had superior intelligence. We can further see in this case the ups and downs in the boy's development owing to the mother's inability to maintain a consistent approach.

PART III

CONCLUSION

Now that you are at the end of this book, you may examine what you have absorbed from it. While you were reading, many thoughts might have passed through your mind, stimulating or upsetting you, as the case may be. This is the time to integrate these thoughts. The process of thinking and re-thinking after you are through will determine what value or use this book has for you.

I hope that one fact was brought home clearly and unmistakably—that it is within your power to bring about happiness and success for your children. I wish you would, then, stop for a moment and consider the larger implications of this fact. While it is only natural that you are concerned primarily with your own family, with your own children, you should not lose sight of the fact that you also hold in the palm of your hand the destiny of mankind. Each generation of parents is the foundation of the future. We cannot establish the extent to which external social conditions and our inner preparation decide the fate of humanity—whether we need first better individuals to form a better society, or a better society to produce better individuals. The two factors work hand in hand: the training of children influences the future social order, just as existing living conditions determine the forms of upbringing. The progressive evolution of mankind is inseparably linked with the improved spirit and technique of child-rearing.

Man's imperfection today is in part conditioned by the training that he has heretofore received.

We have today a dim vision of the road that may lead from this imperfection to heights previously unknown. The hypothesis of the evolution of new social forms, the idea of a great and unlimited expansion of the powers of the human intellect by a control of nature—these find a peculiar confirmation in our pedagogical experiences. A more adequate treatment of man beginning at infancy could completely unfold his creative faculties, and develop capabilities and qualities that now are all but inconceivable. We see only the first glimmerings of the light. But what we already know of the prevalent frustration and repression of the human powers gives us some idea of the myriad potentialities, ethical, intellectual, and emotional, that are obscured by training as hitherto practiced.

The previous belief in the omnipotence of heredity is now shaken. This credence was based on an understandable pessimism arising from the limited knowledge of the possibilities of proper training. Is it conceivable that, for millennia, really false principles of pedagogy were consistently applied? The previous tenets of education were not false; they were but the logical reflection of a culture-era that extends from the beginnings of civilization into our own day and age—an era marked by the conflict of man with man. Outside of our European-American culture there were, and still are, communities of a homogeneous type, tribes and clans which, within their own limits, have scarcely any notion of a hostile, competitive order (other than that involved in the relation of the sexes). Their education often proceeds from a wholly different premise, shuns personal punishment and abasement of children, and corroborates in many respects the experience of modern psychiatry.

It is certain that the shortcomings of the present methods of training have been emphasized by the special obstacles that our own times have laid in the way of parent and child. Yet it is beyond question that good parents, now as always, can discover and apply effectual training procedures. Our new understanding is built on the experience of untold predecessors. Many exceptional men and women, who towered above the general level of their contemporaries, were to a great extent the product of superior upbringing. (If their success were due solely to heredity, we would expect the children of geniuses to take after their parents more often than they do.) Nor is it mere coincidence when a certain graduating class of a high school produces a number of outstanding individuals that far surpasses the average. Here we see evidence of a blessed confluence of effort that is anything but chance, and of a pedagogical skill that has developed potentialities which under other circumstances might have lain fallow.

The extent to which a human being is capable of development can be shown by a simple illustration. If the child of a bushman were early transplanted and accepted into American culture he would develop powers and capacities that he could never possibly have attained in his original environment. Neither hereditary defects nor his assumed or actual inferior brain-development would prevent him from rising far above the norm of his own community. Hence we can conceive that, through better methods of training and improved living conditions, the men and women of the future will exceed our present cultural level as we ourselves exceed the level of primitive peoples. . . . We may well be stepping, right now, on the threshold of a new era of humanity.

Index